Bridging the Divide at Transition:

What happens for young people with learning difficulties and their families?

Pauline Heslop, Robina Mallett, Ken Simons and Linda Ward

Pauline Heslop, Ken Simons and Linda Ward are based at the Norah Fry Research Centre, University of Bristol; Robina Mallett works at the Home Farm Trust

British Library Cataloguing in Publication Data
A CIP record for this book is available from the Public Library
ISBN 1 904082 08 4
© Copyright 2002 BILD Publications
BILD Publications is the publishing office of the
British Institute of Learning Disabilities
Campion House
Green Street
Kidderminster
Worcs
DY10 1JL
Telephone: 01562 723010
Fax: 01562 723029
e-mail: enquiries@bild.org.uk
Website: www.bild.org.uk

Please contact BILD for a free publications catalogue listing BILD books, reports and training materials.

Cover illustration by Angela Martin

Acknowledgements

We are very grateful to the many people who took part in this research project. In particular, we would like to thank the 283 families who completed and returned the questionnaire to us. We are aware that for some people it was a difficult process, both in terms of finding the time to focus on it and because it stirred up emotions about their experiences at transition. Without the commitment of these families the research would not have been possible.

We are also enormously thankful to the 27 young people and their parents who spoke to us at length about their experiences. We are grateful for the time that they gave the project and the openness with which they shared their knowledge and thoughts.

A number of people supported the research. Our thanks to the young disabled people in Southport and Southall for helping us plan how to interview young people. Their insight and expertise was crucial in the design of the guided discussion booklet for young people. Many thanks also to Sarah and Ruth at St Christopher's School, Bristol, who spent time with us piloting a variety of interview materials. They gave us valuable indicators as to which interview materials were most effective.

Our thanks, too, to Pippa Murray and Beryl Jones for stepping in at short notice and conducting two of the young people's interviews each.

The project was informed and supported by a research advisory group of: Sandie Bingley, Robert Gramann, Angela Kindleysides, Steve Morris, Silu Pascoe, Margaret Power, Paul Soames and Stuart Todd; our thanks to them for their advice.

We are grateful to the Community Fund (formerly the National Lottery Charities Board) for funding the research.

Finally, thank you to Fiona Macaulay, Maggi Walton, Linda Holley and all others involved for the administrative and secretarial support at the Norah Fry Research Centre and the Home Farm Trust.

Further information

For further information on the 'Bridging the Divide' project, contact:

Pauline Heslop
Norah Fry Research Centre
University of Bristol
3 Priory Road
Bristol BS8 1TX
Tel: 0117 923 8137
Email: pauline.heslop@bristol.ac.uk
www.bris.ac.uk/Depts/Norah Fry

Robina Mallett
Home Farm Trust
Merchants House
Wapping Road
Bristol BS1 4RW
Tel: 0117 930 2608
Email: Robina@hft.org.uk
www.hft.org.uk

Copies of the summary of this report are available free from the addresses/websites above.

'Growing Up', an accessible leaflet on transition for young people with learning disabilities, is available free from BILD, tel: 01562 723010

All Change: transition and young people with learning disabilities. An information guide – an information pack for parents, professionals and young people is available from Pavilion Publishing, Brighton in early 2003, tel: 01273 623 222 or *www.pavpub.com.*

Contents

Chapter 4 Transitions to adulthood: what makes a difference?

Chapter 5 What makes for a better transition experience?

Chapter 6 Key issues and examples of innovative practice

List of tables

List of figures

List of information boxes

Chapter 1: Introduction

This research project was born out of a growing awareness of the inadequacy of arrangements for young people with learning difficulties to make a planned, effective and supported transition to adult lifestyles and services. It documents the experiences of young people with learning difficulties and their parents/carers at transition, using information obtained from a national postal survey, face-to-face follow-up interviews and visits. It also summarises key factors that contribute to making a 'good' transition experience and documents examples of interesting and innovative practice in this area.

The background to the study

We make many transitions in our lives, but perhaps the one with the most far-reaching consequences is the transition into adulthood. For most young people, the process of moving from childhood to adulthood is a difficult time. The physical aspects of growing up are overlaid by the need to negotiate a complex set of changes in roles, relationships, expectations and status. Not least, the process typically involves huge changes in the environments in which people live (as they move away from the family home) and in which they spend their days.

The process is doubly complicated for young people with learning difficulties who rely, to a greater or lesser extent, on services. As well as the challenges everyone faces, they have the additional problem of managing the move between two sets of services: those for children and those for adults. This is not simply a case of moving from one otherwise similar set of organisations targeted at children, to a parallel entity concerned with adults. The reality is more complex than that: the two sets of services tend to be organised in very different ways and to have very different cultures.

The lack of coordination between children's and adult services has been widely recognised, as has dissatisfaction with transition planning and the arrangements that have been made for young people with learning difficulties as they move towards adulthood. In 1999 the Home Farm Trust (see Box 1) decided to carry out a more systematic review of the experience of parents/carers and young people with learning difficulties, focusing on the extent to which transition planning conformed with legislation and guidance. The University of Bristol's Norah Fry Research Centre (see Box 2) was chosen to act as a partner in the project.

Box 1: The Home Farm Trust

The Home Farm Trust is an organisation founded by parents in 1962. Its purpose is to provide, in consultation with users, residential and other services for people with learning disabilities which develop their potential. The Family Carer Support Service provides newsletters for families, targeted mailings about local services and events, a programme of workshops for families and specific responses to individual queries. Over 1,800 families, from a range of backgrounds and representing a wide geographical spread, are in regular contact with the service.

Box 2: The Norah Fry Research Centre

The Norah Fry Research Centre undertakes applied research into services and supports for people with learning difficulties, including highlighting good and innovative practice, identifying weaknesses and suggesting areas for improvements. The Centre is committed to trying to involve people with learning difficulties in the work it undertakes and to producing findings from its research in accessible formats, as well as working to ensure research findings are disseminated in ways that are most likely to contribute to positive policy and practice change.

The social policy context in England

The Education Act 1993 and the associated Code of Practice on the Identification and Assessment of Special Needs have, until 2001, represented the primary statements of policy in this area.[1] They require that any young person who has a statement of special educational need should also have a transition plan drawn up by the Local Educational Authority (LEA) at the first annual review of their statement after their 14th birthday. New guidance introduced in 2001 specifies that the transition plan should be drawn up at the first annual review of the young person's statement after they have started Year 9 of school.

On the whole, the guidance is both comprehensive and helpful. Although the system of planning is to be driven by schools and LEAs, the guidance makes clear that transition planning is a continuing process that should be concerned not simply with leaving school, but with the move to 'adult life' generally. It stresses the importance of partnership, both with agencies like social services and careers service, but also with parents. Similarly, it is very explicit about the importance of involving the young person in the planning process,

---

1 These have been revised by the Education (Special Educational Needs) (England) Regulations (2001).

requiring the plan to take account of the 'young person's hopes and aspirations':

The views of the young people themselves should be recorded wherever possible in any assessment, reassessment or review during the years of transition. (6.59)

The guidance requires schools and LEAs to 'consider' ways of ensuring young people's views are incorporated, and suggests curriculum planning should focus on:

... activities which encourage students to review and reflect on their own experiences and wishes and to formulate and articulate their views. (6.60)

While the educational issues remain a key part of the transition planning, the process is meant to be much wider in scope, covering all aspects of the young person's development, and *specifically* including topics like self-advocacy, the growth of personal autonomy and the development of independent living skills.

While the Education Act 1993 and the associated Code of Practice represent the primary statements of current policy, a range of other legislation is also particularly relevant to transition services:

• **The Chronically Sick and Disabled Person's Act 1970** sets out a broad range of services that local authorities may make available to disabled people. These services provide the basis for provision under other legislation.

• **The Disabled Persons (Services, Consultation and Representation) Act 1986** requires links between education and welfare services at the end of education. It gives LEAs and Further Education Funding Councils (now the National Learning and Skills Council) specific responsibilities for ensuring students with statements of special educational need are known to social service departments and that plans are made for them.

• **The Children Act 1989** requires local authorities to provide a range of family support services for 'children in need', including disabled children. The local authority is also required to keep a register of disabled children and to identify the extent of need in its area, to publicise the availability of services, facilitate the provision of services by independent providers, and promote inter-agency collaboration.

- **The NHS and Community Care Act 1990** provides the legal framework for community care services, giving local authorities responsibility for the coordination, planning, assessment and arrangement of services for adults with health and social care needs. Young people in transition to adulthood are entitled to an assessment of their needs under this legislation.

- **The Quality Protects Initiative** was launched in 1999 with the intention to transform services for vulnerable children, including disabled children, and their families. Within Quality Protects, effective support for disabled children and their families is a key priority, including further consideration of the transition arrangements for disabled young people moving from children's to adult services. Quality Protects requires local authorities to review their existing transition planning arrangements and develop joint inter-agency protocols to improve their coordination.

- **The Education White Paper Learning to Succeed (1999)** provided a new framework for post-16 learning. It states that there must be an assessment of the education and training needs of any young person, who has a statement of special educational need, in their last year of schooling and that reassessment and monitoring must be ongoing.

- **The Learning and Skills Act (2000)** heralded a complete and radical overhaul of the funding mechanisms for adult and continuing education. A range of existing bodies was replaced by a single entity, the National Learning and Skills Council, which has responsibility for planning and funding all post-16 education. In England, the national body has been supplemented by 47 regional Learning and Skills Councils, who are responsible for local policies and priorities. The Learning and Skills Act 2000 gives the Learning and Skills Councils the specific responsibility to pay attention to the needs of adults with learning difficulties and to promote equality of opportunity.

- **The Connexions Strategy (DfEE, 2000)** introduced a new advice and guidance service for all 13 to 19 year olds. The Connexions Service, which is being rolled out between April 2001 and April 2003, will establish local services in each Learning and Skills Council region. These should ensure that every young person will have a Personal Adviser to assess and secure additional support for their learning needs after the age of 16. Although Connexions is a generic service, people with additional needs will be a priority, and Connexions advisers will become a key part of the transition planning process. Indeed, in recognition of the extended transition period for some young people, support from the Connexions service will extend up to age 25 for people with learning difficulties.

- *Valuing People: a new strategy for learning disability for the 21st century (2001)* is the recent White Paper on services for people with learning difficulties in England. Although primarily focusing on services for adults, it does specifically address the issue of transition. Local Learning Disability Partnership Boards (whose membership should include senior representatives from social services, health bodies, education, housing, community development, leisure, independent providers and the employment service, as well as people with learning disabilities and their carers) will be expected to identify a member with lead responsibility for transition issues, and to be responsible for ensuring that arrangements are in place to achieve a smooth transition to adult life for young people with learning difficulties. *Valuing People* also states the need for effective links between children's and adult services in both health and social care. By 2003, local agencies will be expected to have introduced 'person-centred planning' for all young people moving from children's to adult services, and by 2005 they should be offered a Health Action Plan too.

- *The Education (Special Educational Needs) (England) Regulations (2001)* came into force in September 2001. This revises the Education Act 1993 and the associated Code of Practice. However, the new guidance reinforces the earlier messages that transitional planning should be participative, holistic, supportive, evolving, inclusive and collaborative.

- *The Special Educational Needs and Disability Act (2001)* amends the Disability Discrimination Act and inserts a new part, Part IV, to prevent discrimination against disabled people in their access to education. Separate Codes of Practice are presented for schools and post-16 education providers. These make it unlawful to discriminate, without justification, against pupils in any aspects of school life, and against disabled students and other disabled people in the provision of post-16 education and training and other related services.

In 1994, when the Education Act 1993 and the associated Code of Practice were coming into force, Hirst and Baldwin surveyed a group of disabled young people and compared their experiences with those of their (non-disabled) peers. They concluded that between 30% and 40% of the young disabled people found:

> ... *great difficulty in attaining a degree of independence in adult life comparable to that of young people in the general population ...* (p. 110)

Since then, a number of inspection and research reports have indicated that transition from school into adulthood remains stressful and difficult for young disabled people, despite the evolving legislation and guidance. In 1995, a report by the Social Services Inspectorate concluded that:

> . . . disabled young people and their carers face considerable difficulty in easily accessing all services due to responsibilities being fragmented across different agencies. (p. 45)

and that there were:

> . . . dilemmas about how best to integrate the requirements of different legislation in order to develop effective collaboration at a local level. (p. 45)

A few years later, the National Development Team, in a project funded by the Department of Health, examined issues for positive health in the adjustments to adulthood for young people with learning disabilities. They concluded that:

> . . . while a variety of effective local initiatives were being taken or anticipated, the concerns voiced by parents, managers and professionals indicated that the range of barriers was still formidable. (Pearson et al, 1999, p. 87)

In 1999, Morris researched the transition to adulthood for young disabled people with 'complex health and support needs'. She found evidence that many of these young people experienced:

> . . . a failure of health and social services to meet their needs as they grow into adulthood. They are at risk of being socially excluded by services which segregate them from the rest of society and which pay inadequate attention to needs arising from poor health and/or mobility, sensory, cognitive and communication impairments. (p. 135)

Our study was undertaken at a crucial time. The Education Act 1993 and the associated Code of Practice have been in place sufficiently long so that any problems with implementation can no longer be dismissed as 'teething problems'. At the same time, new legislation and guidance to improve services for young people at transition were being formulated; we hope that the results of this study inform the new developments.

How we did the research

A key development over the past decade has been the increased commitment to consulting and involving people who use services in their planning and development. As researchers, we too are guided by the principle that service users should be involved in projects that might have an influence on their lives. So young people with learning difficulties and their families have been involved as advisers to this project, along with an advisory group of professionals in the fields of health, education, social services, careers and the voluntary sector, together with parents and carers. Their comments and insights have guided this research.

The project was divided into two separate but related strands. Strand 1 was a survey of families and follow-up interviews with a sub-sample of parents and young people with learning difficulties. Strand 2 aimed to identify good or innovative practice nationally, with a series of fieldwork visits to selected areas to document appropriate examples.

Strand 1: a survey of families and follow-up interviews

The aim of the initial survey was to identify to what extent the principles outlined in legislation and guidance were being implemented for young people with learning difficulties and their families at transition. We wanted to find out:

- the families' experience of the transition planning process

- the aspirations of the young people and their families

- the outcomes of the process and

- the extent to which the process and outcomes were geared to the views of the young people and their families.

In order to do this, a self-completion postal questionnaire was developed. It was extensively piloted by family carers of young people with learning difficulties, both with and without a researcher (RM) present, and went through several revisions before the final version was arrived at. It was designed to be as easy to complete as possible. Because we were asking questions of families at different stages in the transition process, the sections concerning young people who were still at school, those who had already left school, youngsters who had received some transition planning and those who had not, were all colour-coded, so that respondents could find their way around the questionnaire with ease. Some of the questions were straightforward and factual and just required a tick-box answer; other questions were open, giving respondents the opportunity to write about their views and experiences in their own words. A contact telephone number was given for respondents to call should they have any difficulties with any aspects of the questionnaire. As a result, one respondent completed the questionnaire over the telephone.

A total of 370 questionnaires were posted to families of a young person with learning difficulties, between the ages of 13 and 25 years, who were on the Home Farm Trust Family Carer Database or had moved into one of their residential services. All lived within England. Of the 370 questionnaires distributed, 283 were returned – a response rate of 76%. The data was coded and analysed using SPSS (Statistical Package for Social Scientists). The analyses in this report that detail the results of the survey are based on 272 questionnaires completed by the parents of the young people in question.[2]

The scope for an in-depth exploration of the views of people about their experiences is necessarily limited when using the medium of a postal questionnaire. Follow-up interviews were therefore planned to allow for additional insights and to provide more extensive case material with which to illustrate the material from the survey. The selection of families to interview was based on 'purposive sampling', i.e. they were selected to represent a range of situations identified in the postal survey. Specifically, the criteria for asking families for a follow-up interview were that:

- they reported particularly good or bad experiences of the transition planning process or

- they reported particularly good or poor outcomes following transition and

- they had stated on the survey return form that they would be willing for the researchers to talk to their son or daughter and themselves about their experiences in more depth.

Within these criteria, we selected those who:

- lived in a variety of geographical locations across England

- were at different stages in the transition process.

The young people selected for a follow-up interview had a range of support needs. We included non-verbal young people with profound learning difficulties and severe and complex health needs as well as articulate

---

2. Eleven of the questionnaires were excluded from the analyses: one because it had no identification number, eight because the questionnaires applied to people with learning difficulties outside the age-range of 13 to 25 years and two because they were completed by professionals directly involved with the young person, not family members. See Appendix 1 for discussion of sample composition.

youngsters with learning difficulties who were able to work independently. No attempt was made to assess their capacities before deciding whether or not to select them for a follow-up interview – which was undertaken a year after the postal survey.

Planning and preparing for the young people's interviews was undertaken in consultation with groups of young people with learning difficulties. Two focus groups were held with young people: one to discuss the topic areas for the interviews, and one to discuss how best to engage young people in the interviews. A variety of materials were then extensively piloted with young people with learning difficulties to determine which were most accessible for use in the interviews. Booklets of different sizes and materials using questions, pictures, symbols and photographs about growing up were all tested with young people with learning difficulties who did and did not use speech as a means of communication.

The final version was an A4 size booklet called *Growing Up*.[3] At the front was space for the young person to stick photographs of themselves at various stages of growing up.[4] The remainder of the book asked questions about growing up and offered pictorial suggestions for answers. The young people indicated their answers using bright stickers and were encouraged to talk further about their choices. At the end of the book, the youngsters could add any further comments that they wanted to about 'growing up'. These were written into their book on speech bubble stickers. At the end of the interview, the young people were given their *Growing Up* books to keep.

A total of 27 face-to-face in-depth interviews were conducted with parents and 27 interviews held with young people with learning difficulties. Most of the interviews were conducted in the families' own home, apart from three, which took place at residential centres. All of the young people were interviewed separately from their parents. One researcher (RM) interviewed the parent(s) whilst another researcher (PH)[5] interviewed the young people in a separate room. One of the young people used Makaton signing as their principal method of communication; another used an alpha talker. Makaton was used in conjunction with speech in a further two interviews. The interviews were tape-recorded for later transcription, apart from two of the young people's interviews. These young people preferred not to have their interviews recorded and so notes were taken of the content of these interviews.

---

3. Appendix 2 explains in more detail how the workbook was developed.

4. Parents were asked to provide photographs to be available at the interview, so that the young people could stick these in their books at that time.

5. Two consultants, experienced at interviewing young people with learning difficulties, conducted four of the young people's interviews.

For two of the young people who had profound learning difficulties the interviews gave little information that was meaningful to the research. Time was spent with these youngsters joining in with activities that they enjoyed and communicating with them using the activities as a medium. With these two young people, and probably a further two others, more information might have been gained from a series of meetings with them, in which the researcher could have become a more familiar figure who was more accustomed to their ways of communicating.

Strand 2: fieldwork visits

We were keen to identify instances where services had begun to address some of the concerns and difficulties that were becoming apparent through the research. Through informal networking, we were able to identify some examples of good or innovative practice at transition. Fieldwork visits were then made to document them. The projects selected had to meet the following criteria:

- they addressed issues of concern to young people and their families

- they were designed to increase access to inclusive opportunities and/or address barriers that exclude young people with learning difficulties

- the processes involved were generally empowering for the young people

- they should be relatively unusual and should have been recognised as representing some degree of positive innovation

- they should be person-centred i.e. they should respect people's rights, provide opportunities for self-determination, and support personal development and relationships.

In the end, we selected 10 projects in a variety of geographical locations across England that demonstrated a range of service provision. Each fieldwork visit lasted up to a day. Discussions were held with key personnel in the project and, where possible, a small number of (young) people using the service. Where appropriate, some of the provision was observed. Documentation gathered about the project included copies of leaflets and background briefing materials, evaluation or audit reports and progress or annual reports. We made it clear at the outset of each visit that the project was not being evaluated; the intention of each visit was to collect descriptive material about the project that could be used to illustrate their work, for the benefit of others.

Chapter 2: Transition planning in practice

The Education Act 1993 and the associated Code of Practice on the Identification and Assessment of Special Needs, say that if a young person has a statement of special educational need, they must have a transition plan drawn up by the Local Education Authority (LEA) at the first annual review of their statement after their 14th birthday. At the time of our research, and in anticipation of the revised Code of Practice, this had begun to change to when the young person enters Year 9 of school. The plan should be reviewed on an annual basis and should cover what will happen after the young person reaches the age of 16.

Young people with no transition plan

Although a transition plan is a requirement for young people with a statement of special educational need, we found that in practice only two-thirds (67% n = 60) of those still at school who were aged 14 or over[6] had one. For over a quarter of youngsters (27%) there had been no planning as far as their parents knew. About half of the latter believed this was because the young person was still too young, or they anticipated school-based planning would take place at some time in the future. Others gave particular reasons for the lack of a plan, such as a change of school or changes occurring in other services.

A fifth of the young people (n = 33) had already left school when the Education Act 1993 was implemented (September 1994); at that stage a transition plan would not have been a formal requirement for those youngsters with a statement of special educational need. However, the majority (75%) of young people in the study who had left school had done so after 1994 and therefore *should* have had a transition plan under the terms of the Education Act.[7]

Of those who had left school after the end of 1994, one-fifth (23) had had *no* planning for their future (or at least their parents were not aware of any). Twenty-one of these young people had a statement of special educational need and therefore *should* have had a transition plan. The proportion of young people with no planning might have been expected to reduce over time, as implementation of the Education Act and associated Code of Practice became more widespread. However, although the proportion of young people

---

6. 99% of the young people still at school had a statement of special educational need.

7. 95% of the young people who had left school at the time of the survey had had a statement of special educational need.

with no transition planning did decline from 1996 to 1998, the proportion of young people reported to have had no transition planning before they left school *increased* again between 1998 and 2000 (see Table 2.1). The numbers involved are small; nevertheless, it would appear that, from the perspective of parents, young people with learning difficulties are continuing to leave the school system without any recognisable form of planning, despite legislation and guidance to the contrary.

Table 2.1: The proportion of young people with statements of special educational need who received no transition planning (or any that the respondents were aware of), by year of leaving school

Year of leaving school	Number leaving school	% with no transition planning (or don't know)
Before end of 1994	31	39
1995	16	25
1996	24	33
1997	27	11
1998	22	5
1999	23	13
2000	12	17

Two-thirds of the families whose youngsters had received no planning before leaving school could suggest a reason why this had been the case. Some reported that the young person had left school earlier than expected and had thus missed out on any planning that would usually happen in the last year at school; others said that there was a lack of interest in planning for transition by staff, or that it was not viewed as being the responsibility of the school; while others gave more specific reasons, such as illness, the fact that the young person was in an out-of-borough placement or changes to local services.

A need for transition planning?

The majority of parents (93%) of young people aged 14 or over and still at school, thought that there *was* a need for school-led planning, (even though their youngsters were not receiving any). Some parents felt that plenty of time was needed to prepare for what would happen when the young person left school or because the young person themselves could only cope with change slowly:

Mark[8] is very fearful of change and gets very distressed and sometimes physically aggressive when he is not in control. Needs to know enough about a situation to cope. Therefore, he needs a well-thought out, tailormade (as much as possible) very gradual introduction to change.

Others thought planning was important as schools were best placed to provide help, support and knowledge because of their past experiences with other pupils:

Schools have experience of past pupils going on to various colleges or places of employment. There are few people able to help other than school.

A similar picture emerged with the young people who had already left school *without* any planning having taken place, where 87% of families expressed the need for school-led planning. Again, some emphasised the importance of there being plenty of time for the planning process:

I understand the social services have to oversee arrangements and a care manager has to be appointed. As this takes ages, plans must start early.

Parents sometimes need to be encouraged to think about the future before the final school year.

Others felt school-led planning was important because they had had such a struggle themselves and could have done with the support that school-led planning could have offered:

You need to be a pretty proactive parent to understand/seek out/evaluate exactly what your options are. Schools could operate a valuable service in this area.

We haven't necessarily known who to turn to, whereas school should know all the options.

One parent highlighted what had happened to her daughter because of the lack of planning for her future:

Four years on, and Abigail still does not read or write – and is in a dead-end situation . . . where quite honestly she has deteriorated . . . and that once lively, happy person seems a very long way off.

---

8. All names in this report have been changed to protect confidentiality.

What should planning be about?

All those who thought that there was a need for school-led planning (even though their son or daughter had not themselves had any planning) were invited to say which of 19 topics they thought should have been covered in any planning for their youngster. Table 2.2 shows the findings. The proportion of respondents wanting each of the topics covered was broadly

Table 2.2: The proportion of those who had received no transition planning and the topics that they thought should be/have been covered in school-led transition planning, by whether the young person had left school or not

Topic	% who thought that the topic should be/have been covered in school-led transition planning	
	Of those still at school (n=42)	Of those who had already left school (n=40)
Leisure and social opportunities	86	80
Information about benefits	76	70
Future housing options	76	65
The transfer to adult social services	76	55
Transport to any post-school provision	76	48
Opportunities for further college education	74	70
Independent living skills	74	65
How to plan future goals	71	63
The transfer to adult health services	71	58
Short break provision/respite care	62	55
Managing money	60	60
Adult sexuality/relationships	60	60
Careers and employment after leaving school	48	43
Speaking up for oneself	45	63
Careers and employment long-term	43	50
Counselling advice	33	40
Obtaining aids or equipment	24	20
Housing adaptations	24	8
Citizenship e.g. voting, the law	21	33

similar for those still at school and those who had already left school, with a few exceptions.

Most respondents wanted information about leisure and social opportunities, benefits, future housing options, the transfer to adult health and social services, opportunities for further college education, independent living skills and how to plan future goals. In addition, approximately three-quarters of those with a child still at school also wanted planning to cover transport to any post-school provision. A greater proportion of respondents whose child had already left school (compared with those with a child still at school) would have liked planning to have covered young people learning how to speak up for themselves. These findings show a clear consensus on the issues that those with parental responsibility would value being addressed during transitional planning and suggest additional points for discussion not covered by the questions listed in the Code of Practice 1994.

Further comments about the transition planning process

All the parents of the young people were invited to add other comments about the transition of their son or daughter from school to adulthood. Many of the parents of the young people who had received no transition planning commented on how difficult the experience had been and criticised the lack of support that had been available. Such views were epitomised in the comments of this parent:

> *Almost everything concerned with my daughter's education and different possibilities for life beyond school I have had to find out for myself, through friends and searching through different organisations. It at times has proven to be a long and painful experience. At no time has information been readily available.*

Young people who had some transition planning

Age at the start of transition planning

At the time of the research, legislation directed that young people with a statement of special educational need should have a transition plan started at the first annual review of their statement after their 14th birthday. Figure 2.1 shows the average age the young people were when they started the transition planning process, by their current age.

Figure 2.1: Age at starting transition planning, by current age

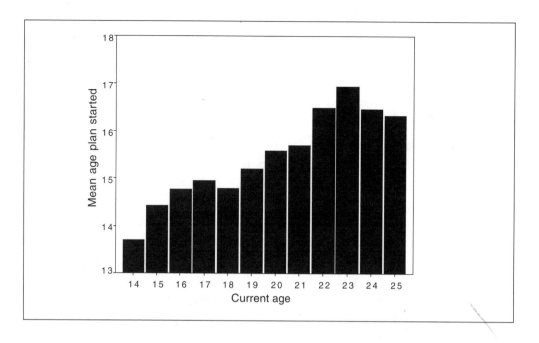

Figure 2.1 clearly shows that older youngsters in the survey were likely to have started transition planning at a later age than the younger people involved. The mean age at the start of transition planning for those still at school at the time of the survey was 14.8 years, whereas for those who had already left school it was 15.9 years. Although there may be some memory bias involved here, the data do suggest that transition planning has started at an earlier age in recent years.

Involvement of the young person in planning their future

Legislation and guidance directs that the transition plan must pay attention to the young person's perspective, and that the views of young people themselves should be sought and recorded wherever possible in any assessment, reassessment or review during the years of transition (Education Act 1993, and the associated Code of Practice on the identification and assessment of special needs, Sections 6.59 – 6.60). Indeed, ways of encouraging student decision-making during transition are suggested in the Guidance (Section 6.60). Similarly, the Children Act 1989 states that there is a duty for social service departments to involve all children/young people that they are in contact with in planning their futures. The questionnaire was designed to investigate the extent to which this was happening. Figure 2.2 illustrates the results.

Figure 2.2: Involvement of the young person in planning for their future

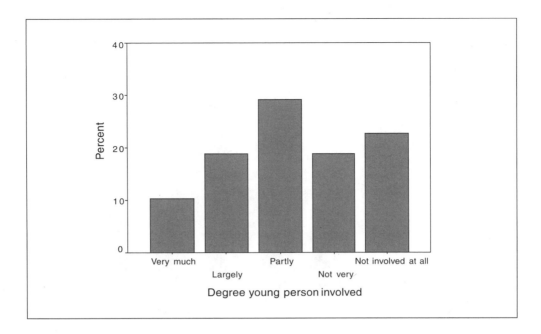

As Figure 2.2 shows, just over a quarter (29%) of the young people for whom transition planning had started, had been 'partly involved' in planning for their own futures, with another 29% 'largely involved' or 'very much involved', according to their parents. Thus, over half (58%) of the young people were reported to have been at least 'partly involved' in the transition planning process. However, this leaves a substantial proportion of young people with little, if any, involvement, including almost a quarter (23%) who were reported not to have been involved at all.

One might expect these proportions to have altered with time as the principles of the Education Act and the Children Act became embedded into practice, and as expertise was gained in involving children and young people in making decisions about their lives. However, we did not find this to be so. The proportion of young people 'not at all' involved in their transition planning (according to their parents) did not differ to any significant extent when the year of leaving school was taken into account. Figure 2.3 illustrates the degree of young people's involvement in the transition planning process, according to whether or not they were still at school at the time of the survey.

As Figure 2.3 shows, those who had already left school were more likely to have been involved in the transition planning process than young people currently still at school.

Figure 2.3: The degree of young people's involvement in the transition planning process, according to whether or not they were still at school at the time of the survey

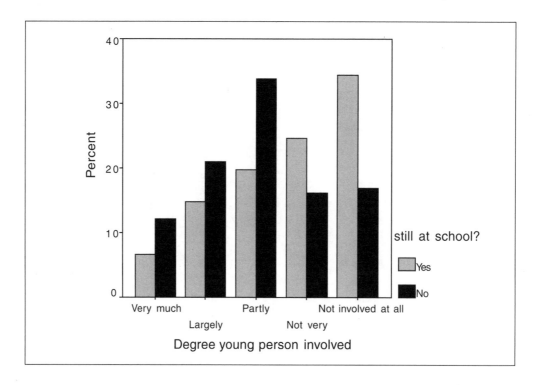

In principle, all young people have a number of rights. The United Nations Convention on the Rights of the Child (covering young people up to the age of 18) states the right of young people to:

> ... *be consulted about any decisions affecting him/her. (Article 12)*

while the Children Act 1989 states that:

> *Even children with severe learning disabilities or very limited expressive language can communicate preferences if they are asked in the right way ... No assumptions should be made about "categories" of children with disabilities who cannot share in decision-making. (Vol. 6, Para. 6.8)*

Yet data from the questionnaires suggest that many young people with learning difficulties, especially those still at school, are not really involved in decision-making about their future lives, despite current national legislation and international guidance. Indeed, questionnaire responses frequently reported that one negative aspect to the planning process for the young person was their confusion and bewilderment at what was happening. Again, this applied both to those who had already left school (11%) and to those who were still at school (20%). Parents reported:

[It was] confusing for her.

He found the process very unsettling and he was bewildered because he did not appear to know what was going on.

He was obviously frightened by the move.

Not enough time spent dealing with the whole issue of moving from school to the training centre. Ken never really understood what was happening.

The 27 interviews with young people provided an opportunity to ask them whether they felt they had been asked what they would like to do after leaving school, and if they felt they had been given choices. Twelve said 'yes' to both questions, three said 'no' to both and in three cases no answers were given. Of the remaining young people, one was unsure whether they had been asked, one said it was 'up to my parents', while six commented that although they were asked what they would like to do they were not given a choice – staying at school/leaving school/going to college/going to a day centre was what they *had* to do.

Why are young people less involved in the planning process than they should be?

There are a number of reasons why young people with learning difficulties may be less involved in the transition planning process than they should be. First, there is the perceived difficulty of facilitating student involvement at planning meetings. Although this was not explicitly asked about in our study, we did find that only a half (52%) of all the young people for whom there had been some transition planning had attended one (or part of one) planning meeting; only two in five (39%) of these young people had directly contributed their views at the meeting – half of these were supported by an independent advocate to do so. The use of independent advocates in supporting young people at planning meetings is a relatively recent, and far from widespread, development. None of the young people who left school before 1994 had this type of support, and no more than a handful of young people had been supported by an independent advocate in each school-leaving year. There was no evidence of an increase in the proportion of young people supported by independent advocates over time, and through the interviews we gained the impression that careers advisers were most likely to have provided this assistance.

For 16 of the 27 parents we spoke to, their son or daughter *had* attended transitional planning meetings. We asked how they had been involved. Sometimes *attendance* had not meant *engagement*:

She would just sit with her head down, it was a job to get her to respond. One to one she was alright but she couldn't take a lot of people all at once.

Parent: *On occasions it was just us, and other times he was present but would often get up and leave the room. He just wasn't listening really, he'd be gazing round the room or wanting to talk about something completely different.*

Interviewer: *Did you feel he had the concept that he was going to be finishing at school and going on to something else?*

Parent: *No, no.*

Some parents recalled feeling concerned about the way that professionals present had taken their son or daughter's contributions at face value without checking what lay behind:

She said she wanted to go to college, but that was because at the time I was at college . . . there were no alternatives spelt out for her, you could do this, that or the other . . . not like planning for the boys [her brothers].

Others had sensed professionals looking for particular responses from their child; this was most frequently reported when the professionals did not have an established relationship with the young person:

It was never that they just spoke to me. They [a careers adviser] did direct questions to her and allow her time to answer . . . but sometimes you have to be careful in that situation because I think they can lead you . . . They sort of tried to steer her.

Others recalled different emotions associated with their son or daughter's participation:

She was about 19. I think that was one of the first times I had experienced her being consulted about her future . . . We found it difficult because she was fidgeting and distracted, and for us it was an important meeting because we were applying pressure because we didn't fancy her going to the local day centre which wouldn't have suited her at all well.

One father described his reactions on hearing his son first declare his interest in going away from home at a planning meeting:

He was at all the annual reviews . . . we wanted him actively involved. He came out with some things that surprised us. He actually told us he wanted to go residential – it came as a huge shock! . . . most of his friends were going residential, we think it came from there. We weren't convinced that's really what he wanted. Over a period of time you begin to realise he really does mean it.

Other research concerning family carers of people with learning difficulties has indicated that the presence of their relative sometimes inhibits carers from raising all the issues on their minds (Robinson and Williams, 2000). This may have been the reason that some young people did not attend their transitional planning meetings. The interviews gave us the chance to ask parents whether this was also a consideration for those whose son or daughter had attended reviews. In general the answer was 'no'; one mother explaining that if there were issues that would have been difficult to discuss in her son's presence there were other times to communicate them. One family did, however, recall discovering it was best to avoid discussions about housing options:

We were always open with her . . . once we did realise it was terrifying her . . . we made our decision quite quickly then didn't we? We were raising her anxieties by talking about it.

Involvement in planning one's future need not necessarily mean just attending or contributing to meetings. Indeed, a number of young people had been invited to contribute their views *outside* the meetings. This was the case for 14% of the young people for whom there had been some transition planning, but who had not necessarily also attended transition planning meetings.

Interviewer: *Do you remember going to any meetings when you were at school to talk about what you'd do when you left school?*

Respondent: *They used to have annual reviews and parents evening.*

Interviewer: *And did you go to those?*

Respondent: *My parents only did.*

Interviewer: *And did people ask you what you would like to do?*

Respondent: *Yeah . . . It was my idea to go to college.*

It was an ongoing assessment period really. Her teacher had picked up the vibes from her day-to-day discussions with her, because the whole of her last two or three years at school were aimed at moving on to the next stage in their development.

A second factor making it difficult for young people to participate in decision-making about their future lives is the lack of any real choices or options for them.

No options were given other than placement at the local tertiary college.

One recommendation only – no choices or options.

So little choice available post-16.

A number of parents said that this was the least positive thing about the planning process for their son or daughter. Even so, one father, pointing out that the lack of choice made his son's participation in planning his future difficult, still saw value in his son's presence at planning meetings:

It may not be a great amount of choice because he doesn't have enough information, nor do we, we're in the same boat, but at least he knows we're looking at it.

Good practice would suggest that young people should be given the chance to try out options and/or make visits to adult services before leaving school; this had been the case (to date) for only half of the young people still at school. However, this was age-related: almost two-thirds of those over the age of 16 and still at school had made at least one such visit; while over three-quarters (78%) of those who had already left school at the time of the survey had been given the opportunity to try 'link placements'[9] before leaving school, or had made visits to adult services; one young man also mentioned that videos (about colleges) had been helpful in imagining options.

In themselves, link visits may help a young person with learning difficulties anticipate or accept a proposed change of location, but ideally, this should be done in conjunction with discussions with the young person about how s/he felt about the visits. Although such discussions may have taken place in school, in a few cases there seemed to be a lack of communication with parents about link visits. One mother, for example, explained that she had known nothing of the short visits her son had been making 'once or twice a month' to a day centre until she went to a meeting three or four months later,

---

9. Link placements are designed to introduce school pupils to a variety of courses on offer at a further education college. Pupils generally spend half a day to two days a week at college; spending the rest of their time at school. The aim is to prepare young people for entry to further education after leaving school.

so she had done nothing to find out what he felt about the place or discover his understanding about the reason for the visits:

> *I think for him it was somewhere to go for a couple of hours . . . as far as he was concerned that's all he was ever going to do – was just go and visit and go back to school . . . he never came home and said 'Guess where I went today' . . . I mean if we had known, from the very beginning, we could have talked to him about it.*

Others referred with great satisfaction to the way the practical aspects of links had been managed:

> *They took them quite a few times . . . they had to get him on a bus . . . then they'd go by car and shoot to the other end to make sure they all got off at the same stop . . . in the end . . . Geoff used to take the others.*

Having accompanied classmates to the college most local to his school a day a week for two years, one mother described how her son's school had made fresh arrangements for him to get used to the college he had subsequently chosen to attend post-school:

> *He's been going every other week for one day and they're trying to get him used to going . . . he's going with his one to one . . . his school is supplying the minibus for him one day a week – just for him.*

For others, transport problems had become barriers to sampling post-school options:

> *At the beginning of the year he was going to organise all sorts of tasters, wasn't he and nothing happened . . . college suggested it was possible for her to come one day a week . . . to make sure she liked it and then there was something on the funding front . . . partly the transport.*

A number of respondents made comments about other ways that the school had tried to involve the young person in planning for their future. Nearly a fifth (18%) of young people had been put in touch with organisations for disabled people such as Mencap or their local Gateway Club; just over a fifth (23%) had been told about other sources of help, such as booklets on general services, information on residential colleges or an open day for adult services. Others mentioned input from careers services or interviews with members of the adult social services team. However, it is likely that some of these would have been targeted primarily towards the young person's *parents* and have only involved the young person themselves in an indirect way:

Interviewer: *Could he actually read that?*

Respondent: *No, we went through it and talked through . . . even if we'd sat and read it day and night with him, he wouldn't have understood . . . We went through it ourselves and then we cut down to the things we thought he needed to be aware of.*

Did transition plans reflect the young person's own views?

Parents were asked if they thought that the plans for their son or daughter's future reflected the young person's own views. Twelve per cent thought not, while a further 17% did not know. Overall, the transition plan was thought to reflect the views, in full or in part, for just over two-thirds of the young people in the survey. There was, however, a marked difference in this between those who were still at school and those who had already left school, as Figure 2.4 shows.

Figure 2.4: **The proportion of respondents who thought that the plans for their son or daughter's future reflected the young person's own views, by whether or not the young person was still at school**

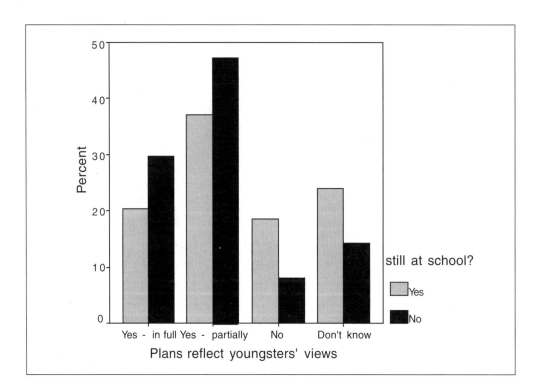

Interestingly, a *smaller* proportion of the transition plans that had been drawn up for the young people still at school reflected their views (in full or part), than the proportion drawn up for those who had already left school. This is a particularly notable finding. Not only are young people still at school *less* likely to be involved in drawing up their own transition plans, but they are also *less* likely to have their views reflected in their plans, when compared with those who have already left school. Young men who were still at school were more likely to have their views reflected in their transition plans in full, than were young women. However, the numbers involved here are very small and must therefore be treated with caution.

Parental involvement in transition planning

Partnership with parents is one of the fundamental principles of the Code of Practice, which recognises that effective assessment and provision will only be secured where there is the greatest possible degree of partnership between parents and their children, schools, local education authorities and other agencies. In addition to this general right to involvement, parents have specific responsibilities and entitlements to documentation. The local education authority is obliged to invite the young person's parents to annual review meetings and to send them a copy of each review report; the transition plan should document parental expectations for their child, what the parents can contribute towards helping their child move closer towards an adult lifestyle, and what the parents' own support and practical care needs will be. After all transition planning meetings, the transition plan should be copied to the parents.

The majority of parents (66%) reported that they felt involved in planning for their son or daughter's future a lot, as opposed to a little (32%) or not at all (2%). There was no significant difference in this between those parents whose son or daughter had already left school, and those whose youngsters were still in school.

Table 2.3 compares a number of different aspects of parental involvement in school-based planning, comparing the proportions of parents whose sons or daughters had already left school at the time of the survey, with those whose youngsters were still at school.

The majority of parents reported that they had been directly invited to contribute their views to the transition planning process and almost three-quarters stated that the planning process had been explained to them. However, after this positive start, there seemed to be little follow-through. For example, only just over a half had been sent copies of minutes from the planning meetings and only two-fifths had received a copy of a written plan for their son or daughter's future, or were invited to comment on a draft plan before it was finalised.

Table 2.3: Aspects of parental involvement in transition planning meetings, by whether the young person had left school or not

Aspects of parental involvement in transition planning meetings	% of young people	
	still at school (n = 61)	already left school (n = 127)
Directly invited to contribute views	85	80
Given enough notice to prepare for planning meetings	72	69
The planning process was explained at the start	71	61
Invited to attend meetings at convenient times	69	72
Invited to attend meetings in convenient places	64	61
Copies of relevant reports had been sent ahead of the planning meeting	56	49
Copy of the minutes from the planning meetings sent	54	50
Received a copy of a written plan for their son or daughter	41	53
Invited to comment on a draft plan before it was finalised	39	45

During interviews it emerged that many parents had not felt satisfied with the way meetings were arranged or conducted. Sometimes this was to do with the school's lack of knowledge or way they handled reviews:

> *He said he didn't think it* [the statement] *carries on but he didn't know what replaced it. He hadn't a clue. Well, to me he ought to have.*

> *I had to take time off work . . . and you* [husband] *didn't hardly attend any did you because you can't just get the time off can you? . . . they were all on a, whatever day it was, Tuesday and that's it. They all followed each other, we felt we were always rushed . . . it was only 20 minutes . . . we all came out thinking, well we want to discuss more and we just couldn't.*

> *The school itself exists in that kind of bubble. It doesn't have much in the way of contact with the real world outside and whilst they go through the process of reviewing situations of individual children, it does feel as if, to some extent, it's just going through the motions.*

In other incidences it was non-school staff who prevented the planning meetings from achieving what was needed:

> *Social services didn't want to travel.*

> *This woman* [the manager of the post-school service recommended by the school] *just looked blank. She* [the head] *said to her 'You have read*

the report on John haven't you?' and she said 'Well, actually no . . . I've been pretty busy at the weekend and I haven't had the time'. And then, all of a sudden, she said, 'Well, I'm really sorry, I've got to go now because I have another meeting'.

Parents need access to information about possible post-school options, both so they can inform their youngster and to allay their own concerns as they contemplate their child's future. We therefore asked about other ways, in addition to transition planning meetings, that parents might have gained access to information helpful in supporting their son or daughter in making decisions about their futures, as Table 2.4 indicates.

Table 2.4: Other ways (in addition to transition planning meetings) that parents had gained access to information helpful in supporting their son or daughter, by whether the young person had left school or not

Parental access to information	% of young people	
	still at school (n = 61)	already left school (n = 127)
Parents' own need for information recognised so that they could help their son or daughter with their options	44	40
Provided with information about appropriate carers groups or forums	25	19
Provided with written information about a range of relevant adult services	21	24
Invited to visit a range of relevant adult services	18	32
Invited to workshops run for family members	15	9
Any other involvement	38	39

Less than half the parents who were aware of transitional planning while their son or daughter was at school reported that their own need for information – so that they could help their son or daughter consider their options – was recognised. Fewer than a quarter reported that they had been provided with written information about a range of relevant services. Parents with young people still in school were more likely than those of youngsters who had already left school to be provided with information about appropriate carers groups or forums, or to be invited to workshops run for family members. They were, however, only half as likely to have been invited to visit a range of adult services themselves, compared with the parents of youngsters who had already left school (although this may well have been an arrangement that would be made later on for the young people still at school).

Over a third of parents reported other ways that they had been involved in planning for their son or daughter's future whilst their child was still at school. The majority of these involved the parents taking control of the situation themselves and doing all the 'running around'. This was particularly the case for those who had most recently left school:

> *I contacted social services transition personnel and the benefits agency. I organised this. I was not invited to do so.*

> *I pressed them and found out by myself what was available, and then fought for it! No social service person helped, only hindered.*

> *No-one actively consulted us or offered options. We undertook our own research, explored options etc.*

The interviews provided much evidence of the responsibilities parents carried at this stage of their son or daughter's life. In anticipating, planning for and managing through times of change, they mentioned ensuring the accuracy of reports, making information accessible to their son or daughter, using holiday leave to visit possible provision, suggesting new approaches and solutions to the school, advocating for the right services, keeping their son or daughter's social and leisure opportunities going, providing access to opportunities that develop independence as an investment for the future, being available to provide care because services were not available every week day, coping with uncertainties about funding and vacancies, learning how things work and encouraging various agencies to speak to each other. Where transitions from school had not been successful parents were often haunted by a sense of failing their son or daughter:

> *With hindsight I feel terribly guilty about sending him there but I was advised by the school that this was definitely the best place . . . no question about it . . . I mean when we think about it we think 'Oh God. We did him such an injustice sending him to that' . . . but we went on . . . we thought well, they're the experts, they must know.* (Parent of a young man who changed from being 'outgoing', 'would . . . get up on the stage and perform', 'absolutely loved life' to someone who could barely leave the house following an unsuccessful placement)

> *I mean, in hindsight, the best thing would have been to send her to [college] . . . but I didn't realize I could have asked for more support.* (Parent of a young woman who had not known about a new course at a particular college for which there would have been transport provided

– until after her daughter had begun a college course requiring the use of public transport on which she was sexually assaulted)

Several mentioned feeling they were penalised for being proactive:

I think with a middle class family we're seen to be coping and that, by and large, when that's the case, they let you get on with it . . . you either have to abuse them or have a complete breakdown. That's the only way you get anything.

I had the audacity to go round and look at things myself and not leave it to the school and I think it got her back up . . . I think she thought 'well you know what you're doing, go and find a place for her then'.

Interviews confirmed that talking to other parents and membership of disability groups furnished much helpful material in information seeking:

Helen [another mother of a learning disabled daughter] *has been so useful . . . she's told me loads of things: what to look out for, and do this and do that . . . she's got a file that thick of things . . . I belong to Mencap as well.*

We get together and discuss, because we all go through this . . . at the same time . . . we know we're not going to get a lot of information so . . . it's just a networking process for us.

A holistic approach to planning?

The transition plan itself is supposed to draw together information from a range of individuals, within and beyond the school, in order to plan coherently for the young person's transition to adult life. This implies a holistic approach to planning, and the working up and implementation of a transition plan that touches on every aspect of the young person's future life: living arrangements, personal and social life, well-being, education, training and work. Table 2.5 details how well the planning process had dealt with a number of these different aspects of young people's lives, for those still at school and for those who had already left school.

Table 2.5 reveals a stark mismatch between the most frequently reported topics that families of those who had received *no* transition planning *wanted covered* (Table 2.2) and the topics most frequently reported as *having been covered* in transition planning for youngsters. Table 2.2 indicates that approximately three-quarters of those respondents reporting no transition planning whose son or daughter was still at school thought that:

Table 2.5: The proportion of respondents who thought that the planning process dealt with different aspects of young people's lives 'well' or 'partly'

Issues	% of respondents who thought that the issue was/is being dealt with 'well' or 'partly'	
	Young person still at school (n = 61)	Young person has already left school (n = 127)
Opportunities for further college education	74	81
Independent living skills	63	78
Adult sexuality/relationships	60	59
Careers and employment after leaving school	52	40
Speaking up for oneself	49	50
Leisure and social opportunities	47	38
The transfer to adult social services	36	58
Managing money	38	56
Transport to any post-school provision	30	48
Housing adaptations	37	33
Information about benefits	26	40
The transfer to adult health services	28	33
Future housing options	27	27
Careers and employment long-term	19	19
Obtaining aids or equipment	17	17
Counselling advice	15	21
Citizenship e.g. voting, the law	10	14
Short break provision/respite care	10	8

- leisure and social opportunities
- information about benefits
- future housing options
- the transfer to adult social services and
- transport to any post-school provision

ought to be covered in transition planning. By contrast, the five topics that were most frequently reported as covered by those still at school who *had* received transition planning were (see Table 2.5):

- opportunities for further college education
- independent living skills
- adult sexuality/relationships

- careers and employment after leaving school and

- speaking up for oneself.

For those who had already left school the differences were rather less stark, but nevertheless noteworthy. The five topics people most frequently said would have been useful were:

- leisure and social opportunities

- information about benefits

- opportunities for further college education

- future housing options and

- independent living skills

whereas the five topics most often reported as having been covered by families whose youngsters had already left school were:

- opportunities for further college education

- independent living skills

- adult sexuality/relationships

- the transfer to adult social services and

- managing money.

So the expectations and needs of parents for particular topics to be covered in transition planning were often quite unlike the *actual* topics that were reported to have been covered by those who had received some planning. For example, over half of those whose child received no transition planning when they were at school thought that discussions about short break provision or respite care would be important to cover, yet fewer than 10% of those who received transition planning thought that this had been covered 'well' or even 'partly'.

Recognising that the age of the young people might be a factor here (as some of the young people at school were still only in the early stages of transition planning) the data was re-analysed for those in their anticipated final year of school. Only eight of the young people for whom there had been some school-led planning were in their final year, so these results do need to be interpreted cautiously; nevertheless they support the findings above. For those young people in their final year at school for whom there had been some transition planning, half or more of the parents reported that the following issues had *not* been dealt with at all: transfer to adult health services (seven out of eight parents), changes in benefits/claiming benefits (seven), future housing options (six), short break provision/respite care (five) and transport to any post-school provision (four). Three of these topics (information about benefits, future housing options and transport to any post-school provision) were, as we have seen, among the five topics that those whose children had received no transition planning when they were at school most often said should have been covered.

Table 2.5 highlights that where there had been some transition planning it had very largely been about opportunities for further college education. Independent living skills, adult sexuality/relationships, managing money and the transfer to adult social services were the only other issues reported to have been dealt with 'well' or 'partly' by more than half the parents by the time their son or daughter had left school. However, given that most support services for disabled adults are accessed through Community Care Act assessments undertaken by adult social service teams it is worrying to find that 42% of those in our survey left school with their families considering this had not been dealt with at all. Our interviews also revealed that where independent living skills, adult sexuality/relationships, speaking up for oneself and managing money had been covered, this was more likely to have been as part of a 'Leavers' Curriculum', rather than possible future needs in these areas having been talked about at planning meetings.

When asked which topics they would have wanted covered during transitional planning, parents whose son or daughter had had no school-based planning most frequently mentioned issues concerned with the longer term. Table 2.2 indicates that in facing the post-school future most parents are concerned that as they move into adulthood, their son or daughter will have companionship and fun (rather than isolation or total dependence on the family for all 'extra curricula' activities), financial independence, suitable accommodation and support from adult service providers. Given the fact that discussions were actually far more likely to deal only with the immediate move to post-school educational provision (see Table 2.5), we asked those we interviewed how they felt about the apparent short-termism of planning during the school years. It seemed that many believed it was too early to begin imagining future possibilities:

> **Interviewer:** *At school there wasn't any talk about future housing options, or leisure and social opportunities or transfer to adult social service?*
>
> **Respondent:** *Not at school no.*
>
> **Interviewer:** *Do you think that would have been useful to know about, early on?*

Respondent: *Not particularly at 16. I think when she was in her second year of college, yes.*

Interviewer: *It looks as though the main thing they dealt with was actually the next college placement and there wasn't much talk about housing for the future or involving social services or anything like that . . . do you think that would have been useful?*

Respondent: *I think it would have been useful but not necessarily at that point.*

Interviewer: *You said careers and employment were only partly dealt with but that was mainly because you wanted the emphasis that was most relevant to you, to plan just for the next stage . . . and not discuss much more beyond that.*

Respondent: *Exactly! Because I felt by the time we got to that stage the information would have been different anyway . . . I didn't want to waste their time or mine.*

However, knowledge about the structure of services might help allay some parents' concerns:

Interviewer: *Do you think it would have been useful to have been signposted to someone who could explain the benefits situation . . . and that you acquired adult social services via an assessment called the Community Care Assessment. . .?*

Respondent: *So much of that was . . . you find out from other parents . . . you know somebody finds that benefits have changed . . . we learnt a lot that way. But no, having somebody explain it would have been much better.*

Transition planning as a process

The process of planning for the future is meant to be an evolving one, with recognition that leaving school is just one step along the path of a longer journey. Subsequent annual reviews are as important as the first, although the procedures for these reviews are not explicitly addressed in the Code of Practice. A number of parents commented on the importance of seeing transition planning as a *process*, not an isolated, annual event.

A third (33%) of the respondents whose son or daughter was still at school stated that one of the most positive aspects of the planning process for their son or daughter was connected with *visits*, over a period of time, to possible future options. These included visits to colleges, work experience placements and day centres. One parent summed up the most positive aspects of the transition planning process for her daughter as being:

That she has a sense of something being appropriate for her, even though not sure yet what it'll be . . .

and another that their son was:

. . . given ideas about what may be possible for him in the future.

These comments were generally echoed by the group of respondents whose sons or daughters had already left school. Again, a third (32%) of these respondents stated that one of the most positive aspects of the planning process for their son or daughter was connected with visits, over a period of time, to possible future options, or to *the length of time itself that was allowed for planning.* For example, one parent stated that her daughter was: ' . . . able to sample possible placements in good time for final selection to be made', while another emphasised that their child wasn't 'under any stress', was able to take things 'one step at a time so [he] wasn't confused by it all', or commented positively on the 'very gradual transition'.

Only a few respondents said that for them planning had been a single event, *not* a process, with little subsequent coordination between the different agencies involved. One parent said that:

Once done, the plan was virtually ignored!

and another:

I would like to see more involvement in plans and not just at annual reviews and more firm plans made for his future rather than going from one year to the next not knowing what the longer term plans might be.

Other comments

All the parents who responded were invited to add other comments about the transition of their son or daughter from school to adulthood. For some of the young people who were still at school the transition process and planning were still in their early stages; so for those still at school, the responses have been analysed according to the number of years a young person was still anticipated to remain at school.

Those still at school

As might be expected, most parents of young people likely to stay in school for the longest period (for a further five or more years) felt vague and unsure about the transition planning process that they had experienced to date. One parent commented that there was 'nothing to say yet!' and another that they found it difficult to assess the process at this early stage. Another suggested that they felt their son was 'too young for us to be seriously thinking of the time after school' (Parent of thirteen-year old).

Some of the respondents with youngsters who had another three or four years at school also acknowledged that they were just at the beginning of the process of transition planning and that it was too early to state an opinion. For others who were only in the early stages, transition planning had already been an unsatisfactory experience:

It is early days . . . we only completed the first transition meeting in April. However, I am disappointed – I didn't feel the queries and questions I had were adequately dealt with, nor have I had any written confirmation of what transpired at the meeting. (Parent of fifteen-year old)

To date, this process has been lacking, unsupportive and mostly distressing for all concerned. (Parent of sixteen-year old)

A few had mixed feelings about their experience of planning:

I feel that school have done a lot to help, but where planning 'falls down' it is the fault of social services . . . they give us the impression of being totally uninterested in my son, as if he's a problem that will disappear if they ignore it. (Parent of sixteen-year old)

The largest group of young people still at school were those due to leave in one to two years time (37). Of these parents, most chose not to make any additional comments (62%) but those that did reported varied experiences. For some, the transition planning process was still 'a bit vague' or non-existent (one parent wrote that the social worker had told them that their sixteen-year old son appeared to have 'fallen off' the transition process). For others, however, the transition planning process had so far been a positive experience, with one parent commenting that it had been handled 'very well' and another that the school was 'trying very hard to get it right'.

Others reported mixed experiences:

Our only problem is the worry of . . . funding. Apart from this, everything else is going smoothly. (Parent of eighteen-year old)

or expressed quite negative views:

I'm beginning to feel as if we are about to step off a cliff! . . . anything other than agreement to what is available rather than what would suit seems to be unusual! (Parent of eighteen-year old)

. . . the whole process is putting an almost unbearable strain on me. (Parent of eighteen-year old)

Eleven young people were in their last year at school, and five of their parents chose to comment further about their experiences. Just one of the five made favourable comments, but even this respondent acknowledged that their experience might be unusual:

We have been very lucky . . . [we] feel sad for parents who have always struggled to support at home and now need a good residential placement; first – due to the scarcity of such good places, second – persuading social services to fund, without a death, severe ill-health etc. (Parent of nineteen-year old)

The other four respondents all made unfavourable comments. One parent had entered into the Complaints Process with their social services department, two mentioned having to force the pace, or push for information themselves, and one stated:

We are extremely worried . . . William has only three weeks left at school and so far we don't know what the future holds for him. (Parent of nineteen-year old)

School leavers

Of those who had already left school, having had some transition planning (127 in all) just 50 respondents chose to add further comments about their experiences of transition planning. Eight of these (16%) reported positive comments:

We had a particularly well-organised and trouble-free transition period. The process of obtaining funding which we feared would be a struggle/fight did not turn out to be so. In fact we had word early, before we left on holiday in July.

A positive experience. Jacqui is happy with what she is doing and that is what you want.

However, approximately a third of the additional comments from this group of parents were negative, encompassing a range of unsatisfactory experiences:

I didn't want her to go to a home so soon, and so far away, but it was the only option open to us.

I went with Martin to the special needs officer at our local job centre and he was most unhelpful. He expected Martin to go for jobs which were totally wrong for his needs and inaccessible due to a lack of transport.

It was a very difficult time. The need to focus on the more negative aspects of my daughter's needs and behaviour in order for her to get a service I found extremely upsetting.

Julie has found 'growing up' very hard . . . She needs consistency in her life, but has had constant changes.

Summary

This chapter has highlighted a number of areas where there seem to be continuing problems in the implementation of official guidance on transition planning. In summary these are:

- approximately a fifth of young people with a statement of special educational need left school without any transition planning (or any that their parents were aware of)

- almost a quarter of young people (23%) for whom there had been some transition planning were not involved at all in making these plans

- the topics parents wanted to be covered in transition planning were not the same as those reported to have been covered by those who had received transition planning

- no more than a handful of young people were supported by an independent advocate each school-leaving year

- transition planning did not seem to be a continuous process with a variety of post-school options on offer.

These are issues that will be returned to in the final chapter, where there will be a fuller discussion highlighting examples where services have begun to address some of the concerns. In the next chapter, we will look at what happens in some of the key transition processes that generally signify the move to full adult status.

Chapter 3: Transitions to adulthood: key age-related transitions

There are a number of key transitions that generally signify the move to full adult status. These are:

- leaving school and entering work or ongoing education
- leaving one's family of origin and setting up a home of one's own
- becoming involved in adult personal relationships and possibly becoming a parent
- becoming an independent adult citizen.

In addition, there are a number of age-related transitions that occur during the late teenage years. Of particular importance to young people with learning difficulties are:

- the move from paediatric health services to adult health services
- the change from children's social service teams to adult teams.

Each of these transitions will be discussed in this chapter. Although the key age-related transitions are covered in separate sections here, they are inter-connected; a good transition to adulthood will depend upon a holistic approach to supporting a young person with the changes that are occurring in their life.

Leaving school – for further education, work or other daytime activities

There have been considerable changes, over the past 20 years, in the pathways that young people might follow upon leaving school: there has been a massive increase in the number of young people who go on to further education and training; the transition to work has become highly problematic with a series of successive recessions and changes in labour market demand; while in many cases, training schemes appear to simply delay the transition to unemployment (Morrow and Richards, 1996).

The young people in our study were engaged in a variety of weekday activities, ranging from school to further education, paid employment and attendance at, or involvement in, a day resource or activity centre. Through our interviews we tried to explore with them and their families how the transition from school to their current usual daytime activities had come about, and the key factors in ensuring a smooth transition.

Moving on from school

Of the young people interviewed, about half said that they had been sad to leave school. For those who had been in the same school from the time they started school until they left at age 16 to19, it seems, understandably, to have been a particularly hard wrench:

> *I did find that* [leaving school] *hard, yes. Because I'd been there 13½ years, since I was three.*

Two young women spoke of being upset or crying. Others said that although they liked school, they also liked moving on, because they had felt bored at school, or just felt ready to do new things:

> *I was glad, yeah. It was something to do with my life. I don't want to stay here and get bored.* (Young man in special needs section of mainstream school)

Two of the young people we interviewed were in their final year at school and were in the process of familiarising themselves with their chosen colleges. The parents of both of these youngsters were full of praise for the efforts that were being made by the schools to ease the process:

> *They do* [really care about the next stage] *. . . definitely . . . they're doing everything to help him, basically, at the school.*

> *She* [the school's headmistress] *started looking at the future and saying well what is going to happen when he leaves school, so we considered various options, she actually took me round to see the various places in the area.*

There seemed to be key elements that contributed to the making of successful transitions from school: visits, over a period of time, to possible future options; the involvement of the young person in reaching decisions about where they were to move on to; the early agreement of funding so that there could be a gradual supported introduction to the young person's new environment; and positive support, encouragement, practical help and information for the youngsters and their families from the school.

Further education

The collapse of the labour market for young people in the 1980s and the corresponding rise in unemployment led to a range of government initiatives, largely focused on expanding further education and training provision for young people. The expansion of further educational opportunities had an important impact on transition experiences, especially for people with learning difficulties. Post-school education became a significant part of many disabled young people's experiences in the 1980s and 1990s (Mitchell, 1999).

Over three-quarters (78%) of the young people in the study who were in their first placement after school were in further education. Of these, almost twice as many were at a residential college than at a day sixth form or college. The proportion of young people moving on to college, or the type of college they went to, varied very little between those who had received transition planning and those who had not.

For many of the young people, their parents felt that it was expected that they would move from school to college en bloc with their peers. In many cases, schools seemed to make choices about the colleges that the young people attended, rather than the young people and their families choosing what might best suit them. Many of the young people, while still at school, went on link courses at particular colleges it was expected they would subsequently attend. Two of the parents we interviewed went through the appeals procedure to get their youngsters into the college of their choice instead. For both of these families, it had been a difficult experience, though both had won the appeals. One mother said that she had been successful by getting hold of a booklet on how to get FEFC funding and making sure that she addressed each of the points it recommended in her letter of appeal. She also enclosed a letter from her daughter written in her own words as to why she wanted to go to that particular college.

Key things that made the transition from school to college easier from the perspective of the young people were: the presence of a friend or someone that they already knew either starting at the college with them, or already being there; and the support of their parents in preparing them for college by visiting it in advance and talking to them about it. One young woman, for example, said that the most helpful thing that somebody had done to help her prepare to go to college was:

> *. . . talk to me about it . . . And I like it when they ask me questions about moving on to new colleges.*

She felt that it was more helpful for such conversations to take place on a one-to-one basis, rather than in meetings, which she did not feel a part of:

. . . on my own is best . . . I do like going to meetings, but I don't like disturbing them in the meeting.

For all but one of the young people we interviewed who were at college full-time, the move from school to college had been difficult in the short-term, but all said that once they had settled in they enjoyed college life. A number of them said that going to college made them feel 'grown up'. Two parents, however, expressed concerns:

We don't properly know what goes on . . . we never saw the curriculum or anything like that.

Sam actually went to college at 16 rather than 19 and that was a decision, I think, that was very much our decision . . . One that I'm not sure about now in some ways. We felt he was mature enough to cope with college, but . . . I don't know if we made the right decision there really . . . maybe we should have stepped back a little bit . . . it would have been helpful if someone had come along and said well, have you really thought about this.

About half of the young people we spoke to were able to talk about what they would do *after* leaving college. Three wanted to get jobs and had clear ideas about what these jobs would be. Two were moving on to further college courses. All seemed to accept the fact that they would be moving on from college eventually, although one young woman said that she felt 'angry' that she would have to leave her present college where she was happy and had lots of friends. Some parents had contemplated the inevitable future move from college at an early stage:

When it was decided that Tim should go to [college], at the last meeting I had with social services et al, it was sort of said 'Well, what happens then after three years?' And as usual, social services said 'Well, we don't know what position we'll be in at that time'.

For other parents, the young person's time at college gave them a chance to take stock and relax a little until thinking of the next change:

We didn't realise Kath could stay at college 'til 25, we only found out about that later on . . . It gives you a breathing space to find out if there is anything else . . . It gives her a chance to develop as well.

Paid employment

For many people, work is one of the main defining roles in their lives. Work provides a structure for the week, delivers the income by which we live and contributes to our social networks. It can also increase our self-esteem and self-confidence and can positively affect the way that other people view us. For people with learning difficulties this can be especially important.

In our survey, we asked about the young people's experience of work since leaving school. Of the 109 young people who had left school, only four had experience of paid work. We interviewed these four young people and their families to find out more.

For two of them paid work had arisen from work preparation or placements whilst at college. Geoff had a work placement with a supermarket firm whilst at college, working first one day a week, then stepping up to two days and then three days a week. When he left college he went for an interview with the company and was offered a permanent post, with his salary supported by Remploy. The supermarket firm felt that Geoff was capable of doing 60% of the work involved in the post, so they paid 60% of his wages and Remploy the remaining 40%. For both Geoff and his mother it was a very positive experience:

> *That was lovely when he got his first wage slip . . . it was the most wonderful moment, he was so proud . . . he was so proud that he was going to get a new uniform and when he came in it was as if someone had given him a hundred pounds or a hundred million pounds . . . he thought it was wonderful.* (Geoff's mother)

Geoff himself was a little more circumspect: 'I do enjoy it' he said, but added that he really wanted to go to university:

> *I can't go because I'm Downs Syndrome, I can't go to university. It's not fair.*

Robert's job arose as a result of a catering course that he completed, although getting on to the course itself had been a chance occurrence for him. His mother explained:

> *I had a friend who had a daughter . . . and* [she] *started to go there. And she absolutely loved it. And my friend told me about it, you see. And she gave me all this bumph about it. She said, 'If ever you need it'. So, as he was coming to the end of college . . . I got in touch with them.*

Transition from the catering course to paid employment had been thoughtfully carried out, with work placements and then a move into permanent employment supported by a 'buddy' set-up.

Of the two young people who had experience of paid employment since leaving full-time education, one was still working, and one had left paid work and gone to college to learn more independent living skills. Both of the jobs came about by chance through friends or local contacts:

> *The hairdressers . . . they'd been perming her hair all these years . . . and she said 'Well, you know, she can always come here' . . . so she started there and it was just great . . . she was very happy.* (Sue's mother)

Adam himself explained what happened when he tried to get help in finding a job:

> *I went to the job centre . . . This bloke helps with special needs . . . and he was pathetic . . . I didn't get anywhere . . . He just didn't want to bother really or help . . . Mum got a bit stressed with it. . . She said 'You're not going back there, He's no good' . . . So I got a job all by myself . . . I got it and I've been there for two years.*

At the time of the interview, Adam was applying for other jobs; he recognised that starting a new job might be quite hard, but was looking for new challenges.

Day services

For young people for whom further education or paid employment is not possible for some reason, day services can play an important role in engaging them in other meaningful activities. The Department of Health, in 1992, directed local authorities to think about new and different approaches in the provision of day services. The aim was to move towards personally planned programmes of day activities offering social, educational, vocational and leisure opportunities using ordinary community facilities wherever practicable. Progress along these lines, however, has been slow. The Report of the Mental Health Foundation Committee of Enquiry in 1996 suggested that the experience of people with learning difficulties in day centres was varied but that overall, 'Day centres often do not offer what might be seen as meaningful day activities' (p. 38). More recently, the White Paper *Valuing People* (DoH, 2001) reiterated that overall progress has been too slow. It introduced a five-year programme to support local councils to modernise their day services with the aim of ensuring that resources are focused on 'providing people with learning difficulties with new opportunities to lead full and purposeful lives' (7.25).

Fewer than a fifth of the young people (16%) whose parents answered our questionnaire had attended a day centre as their first placement after leaving school. A further 10% had attended a day centre as their second or subsequent placement. Day centre activities were therefore used by approximately a quarter of the young people in our study.

For 11 of the young people we interviewed, daytime activities mostly revolved around day resource and activity centres, combinations of college and day centres or other ad hoc arrangements involving day centre activity in part. Some of the activities were based at the residential placements in which the young people lived. Other young people attended different centres for the different activities that they were interested in.

All but one of the young people had moved to day resource and activity centres *after* a period at college. For some of these youngsters, their time at college had been curtailed because they were not considered to be making sufficient progress, either for the college itself or to satisfy their funders:

> *I think if the Educational Funding Council hadn't withdrawn, threatened to, well they said they were withdrawing at that point, things might have gone more smoothly.*

> *At the end of the day it was a mutual decision that she would have got nothing from the third year there . . . we pulled her out of the college. We didn't let her complete her second year . . . we started looking around. . .[for] something that would better suit her needs . . . we did the ground work.*

In these cases the transition from college to other day services had been problematic; partly due to the time constraints that parents felt they were working within, and partly because they felt that they were left to do the work of investigating and visiting possible placements themselves with little support.

However, even when the young people did finish their college courses as expected, planning for 'what comes next' still seemed to be a last minute scramble for some, with little time to prepare the youngsters for their next move into day services:

There was nobody to say 'this is the next step along the line' or 'you've got this, this and this option'. You know? And it was just up to us . . . it was sort of like the end of the line and, you know, there's no-one to suggest anything else . . . We just lurched . . . the week is put together, but it's . . . we never know where he is.

She came back to nothing . . . nobody was interested at all . . . it was like nothing had ever happened.

Other young people fared better. Parents who reported good experiences in the transition from college to other daytime activities had found the following things valuable: having plenty of time to prepare both themselves and their youngsters for the next step; good communication between the college and parents, both verbal and written in the form of a diary of achievement or something similar; the provision of relevant information for parents; a supportive, helpful approach from the college staff; receptive staff and a degree of flexibility at the services that were under consideration for the next move.

Some of the young people, when talking about their daytime activities said that they felt 'bored', or that they would like to do additional activities such as learning how to use a computer, or first aid. Others were very positive about how they spent their days and were definite that their current activities were what they wanted to be doing. Only a couple of the youngsters mentioned things that had made the transition to day services a good experience for them: visiting a variety of places and trying a number of activities before making their final choice; and allowing plenty of time for them to settle in.

A home of their own?

Patterns of leaving home have changed considerably over time and vary according to age of entering paid employment, age of marriage or partnership, the influence of social policies on housing, education and benefits and the influence of social class, gender, ethnicity and notions of kinship (Morrow and Richards, 1996). This is a transition that is generally becoming harder for young people to achieve and one that requires more parental support than previously. Nowadays, young people may return home several times before finally making the transition to their own homes.

Almost three-fifths (58%) of the young people in our study who had left school at the time of the questionnaire still lived at home. Some of these young people attended residential college, returning home during the holidays or at weekends. Others lived at home full-time.

Most young people expect to leave their families of origin and set up home independently from their parents. Indeed, this is what is generally anticipated of them. For some of the young people that we interviewed who were still living at home, this was also the case:

> *I'd like to go away from home, yes. Do my own thing.*

> *Soon yeah . . . I think I'd like to have a flat of my own.*

> *I'd like to live on my own.*

> *I'd like to live permanently round here* [but not at home].

Others, however, were not so sure or were against the idea of moving on:

> *I don't know. Probably in the future yes, but I'm not quite sure.*

> *I don't know. I might go, but I don't know yet . . . I like staying here 'cos this is my house, you see . . . and it's good.*

> *Living with my parents . . . I like that, it's good. I'd like to* [move out one day] *but I'd have to think about it and talk it over with my parents.*

> *If they* [parents] *can't cope, they will have to put me in a home of some sort . . . I wouldn't want to do that really.*

Only one young woman (out of the 17 young people we interviewed who were still living at home) said that she had never thought about the issue of leaving home:

> *I don't ever think about it.*

Ten of the young people we interviewed had already left their parental home and were living elsewhere. All but one of these were in residential placements. Many of these young people described difficult experiences in their transition from home:

> *It was hard moving away from home . . . moving away to a different area . . . it's hard to leave my mum and dad behind.*

Its really weird. You know, strange.

[It's been scary] *because of moving away from home and that.*

It was upsetting . . . my dad was fluffing up cushions . . . my mum was bawling her eyes out . . . then I was upset because I didn't want to come here, but I do now . . . It was a big step for me . . . I was ever so homesick . . . I feel alright about it now because I have got used to it.

For young people with learning difficulties there are barriers over and above those that other young people have to face. Generally, the likelihood that they will be able to move into appropriate accommodation with the right level of support largely depends on statutory or voluntary sector input. At the time of the study the overwhelming majority of young people were given no option other than some form of residential care. Of the 272 parents who responded to the questionnaire, just one reported that their son was living anywhere other than at home, in residential care or at residential college. His mother had visited residential services assuming that residential care was the only possibility, but had later found out that the local authority were not in favour of that type of provision and expected Supported Living arrangements to be set up around disabled people leaving home. His mother spoke of long delays in acquiring a flat and weeks of hard work when her son and she decorated and equipped it. When we visited him a few months later, Alan was clearly very proud of his own home and very happy with the 24-hour support arrangements that he had there.

Alan's mother was not alone in having to find out for herself, as she went along, what housing options might be available for her son. In our survey, only 11% of parents of young people who had left school having received some transition planning said that future housing options had been covered 'well' in transition planning. Over a half (52%) said that future housing options had not been covered *at all*. It was clear from the responses to our questionnaire, that housing options was a subject that parents wanted more information about. Almost three-quarters (73%) of parents with a young person still at school who had not (yet) received any transition planning thought that future housing options should be covered in transition planning. A slightly smaller proportion (65%) of parents whose son or daughter had already left school without any transition planning thought this too. The lack of information on housing options was reflected in the comments of one parent at interview:

This sounds a bit bizarre really, but, I mean . . . we have no idea of what the process is for him to go into his own form of residence, whether it was sheltered accommodation or in somewhere [residential]. *We haven't got a clue, have we, how that works . . . no idea!*

It was clear from discussions with parents at interview that any 'process' for planning a young person's move from the family home was, at best, vague and ill-defined and more often, a haphazard procedure with uncertain outcomes. A not untypical 'process' was described by one couple:

Mother: *We were only looking, at that point, to perhaps two or three years in the future.*

Father: *We'd heard that they were building two new houses . . . one day, at home, I was feeling so . . . I think it was half term and I was off work and Angie was home. And I thought Oh I am just going to ring Joan and see if the building plans are still on course . . . so I phoned up Joan and I sort of said to her 'I'm just ringing up really to see if the building of the new houses is still sort of due to finish in 2000' And she said 'Well yes, as far as we know. But there's a vacancy coming up at Riverside in a couple of weeks, why don't you go for that?'*

Mother: *So that was when I wrote that letter and said that we'd like to apply for funding. And we went on the list . . . And we waited, and we heard nothing, and we waited and waited.*

[At this time a new keyworker was appointed for their daughter].

Mother: *He was on top of everything . . . he was on the ball . . . he'd say 'How are you getting on with the funding?' . . . He said 'Well, give James Smith a ring. He's the one in charge of funding. Give him a ring. I'll give you his phone number' . . . so he* [husband] *rings him . . . 'Well, I didn't know there was a vacancy' he said 'nobody told me. Oh I didn't realise that' he said 'that puts a whole different complexion on it'.*

Father: *And it happened.*

Mother: *And he said 'We'll hear her case tomorrow' And he did . . . That's exactly what it was: it was a chance phone call.*

Another mother called it 'purely luck' that she had found out about the vacancy in the residential home that her daughter then moved to.

Not all families were as fortunate; one father highlighted how badly wrong things could go, and what the knock-on and longer-term effects of this could be, when there was a lack of coordination leading to one part of the process failing. Because of the 'incompetence and lack of professionalism' of one housing association, a creative arrangement for his son to move into a semi-detached house with two of his friends, also with support needs, fell through.

It sounded like a wonderful arrangement . . . it seemed that the whole deal was virtually signed and sealed and that it would take place in the autumn. It fell through as a result of . . . one of the housing associations . . . who failed to liaise appropriately with the other housing association who were the providers of the house . . . All of them [his son and the youngsters he was going to move in with] had prepared their lives around the idea that this was going to happen. It was just unbelievable . . . he's sort of slipped backwards a bit, he's had other difficulties because this hasn't happened.

The preparation of the young people for the possibility that they might one day move out of the family home seemed to be done largely by their parents, although one young woman said that somebody had come to college to talk to them about living on their own and another father said of the school's input:

In terms of him understanding that he would be moving on that's always been, I think, fairly well done.

Most of the other parents that we interviewed seemed to have been left to undertake this themselves and highlighted the sensitive nature of doing so:

You couldn't go from where we are now to that . . . it doesn't feel we could anyway . . . we'd need stepping stones.

It's not a thing I relish going into because I think she might feel she is being chucked out sort of thing . . . I want somebody, an adviser, to go at it gently and give her the idea to think about.

We had very gently dripped the idea over a period of years . . . that one day it will happen, why it has to happen and why this is the best way to do it . . . we've made her aware that this is a natural progression, that everyone leaves home eventually.

For families where the young person had gone away from home to residential college, the route to a residential home seemed to be smoother. Only a small number of young people that we interviewed were currently at residential college, and each of these parents commented that they would want their son or daughter's next move to be into some form of residential situation away from the family home. All of the parents gave the same reason: that they would not want their son or daughter to lose the skills that they had gained through being in college of living independently of their families. As one mother put it:

It's almost impossible, I find, that when she's home, to let her do things for herself. I mean . . . it's just the way a parent and child relationship is – without even thinking you do things for them.

Of the seven young people we interviewed who had moved away from home (other than at college), four had previously been in residential college. From here, the route to residential care seemed a foregone conclusion. For two of those moving directly from home to residential care, the road was rather less smooth with one of the families having to take their case for residential care to a review panel hearing.

It was evident from our study that families with young people with learning difficulties living at home need both information about future housing options and support with preparing their son or daughter (and themselves) for the transition from the parental home. Their experience was of information that had not been properly collated, and uncertainty about what options could be offered with confidence. For a number of families, finding suitable housing for the young person to move on to had been a matter of chance, of being in the right place at the right time, or of speaking to a key individual with the authority to push things through.

There was little choice of provision available. None of the parents we interviewed had been given more than an extremely limited range of options, if any at all. In only two cases were housing arrangements tailored to individual need – one successfully; the other had failed to materialise. In all of the other families interviewed, the young people had moved into existing provision; there was little suggestion that they had been offered a choice of the kind of housing that would suit them best. If the young people were particularly unhappy with their living arrangements, it was not clear how easy it would be to change them. Mary felt, it was more a case of 'getting used to it'.

Housing transition seemed to be driven largely by the parents themselves, costing them a huge amount of energy and stress. Few felt supported in the process. There was little input from social workers in helping prepare young people and their families for the possibility of living away from home; and there seemed to be even less input from schools or colleges. Housing transitions seemed to be easier for families where the young person had previously attended a residential college. However, the struggle that these families had to secure their son or daughter a residential place at college in the first place seemed to be matched by the difficulties of families trying to get a residential placement when the young person had completed their formal education at school or college. Overall, there seemed to be a lack of partnership working between social service departments and housing agencies at all stages of transition. There was also a constant anxiety on the part of the families that at the next annual review the local authority would challenge the costs of the existing provision or recommend some other type of provision.

The move to more adult social activities, friendships and relationships

As young people grow older and move towards adulthood, participation in leisure and recreational activities, and the positive use of free time, are particularly significant to their mental and emotional well-being. Yet research consistently suggests that young disabled people have fewer opportunities for leisure activities than their non-disabled peers (Morris, 1999; Hirst and Baldwin, 1994; Flynn and Hirst, 1992), and that having something interesting to do with their time is one of the top issues of concern to people with learning difficulties and their carers (Russell et al. 1996). A lack of leisure and recreation opportunities can exacerbate difficulties in establishing and sustaining friendships and relationships, which may be key to combating social isolation and exclusion.

Most of our survey respondents whose son or daughter had received no transition planning, thought that information about leisure and social opportunities should be covered in school-led transition planning (86% of those whose son or daughter was still at school; 80% of those who had left school). Indeed, this was the topic that the largest number of parents thought should be covered. Yet more than half those whose son or daughter *had* received transition planning said that information about leisure and social opportunities had *not* been covered in it (53% of parents whose son or daughter was still at school; 62% of those who had left school). So, families overwhelmingly wanted information about leisure and social opportunities for their son or daughter, but fewer than half were likely to get it.

During the interviews, many of the parents reported having made strenuous efforts to ensure that their son or daughter was involved in leisure or recreational activities. Two had been involved in setting up special youth clubs in their own area suitable for their son or daughter to attend. Others spent a considerable amount of time and energy taking and fetching the young people to and from various activities. As one father explained:

Over the years we've encouraged her to get into all sorts of different things, only to find that she does it for a while and then she loses interest ... we feel that we're forever doing that work 'cos she wouldn't do anything if we just left her.

Rebecca's mother said that she 'hawked' her daughter around the play schemes in the summer:

> *. . . so she is not absolutely bored stiff. She can't go out to play in the street like the other kids so we hawk her around.*

Although most parents tried to get their son or daughter interested in activities with other young people of their own age, some also took their youngsters along to activities that they, as adults, were interested in: one young man went to a model car racing club with his family, another went to a badminton club with his mother and one went to Scouts where his parents were Scout leaders.

During the interviews, all of the young people were able to talk about or demonstrate activities that they enjoyed doing. The most popular activities were those enjoyed by any other young person of their age group: listening to music and following their favourite groups, watching television or videos, watching or playing sport, playing computer games and going to a disco or to the pub. Other favourite activities mentioned included going to special interest or youth clubs, doing art or drama, going swimming or bowling or going to MacDonalds. Few of the young people said that they were bored or dissatisfied with the activities that they did. For example one youngster said:

> *My mum and dad worry about me being bored but I'm not. I make my own amusement. I listen to my music or sleep or watch telly. I'm just quite happy doing that.*

The young people that did express some dissatisfaction with leisure or recreational activities did so for a number of reasons. One commented: 'There's no clubs round here for people like us', adding that if he went to 'ordinary' youth clubs he would 'get picked on', whilst Robert explained that although he might be interested in going along to a new club, he would be put off because of how people would react to him the first time he went there. Abigail said that it was 'hard' that she had had to stop attending a youth club that she had been going to for a number of years because she had become too old. She said that she thought the best way to make new friends was through doing things in her spare time, but that there was no other youth club available for her to attend. The issue of having to stop attending some leisure or recreational activity because of age restrictions was one commented on by a small number of parents when they were interviewed. For example, one mother recounted how her son used to go camping with the Scouts, but that this had stopped when he had reached a certain age, with nothing else to replace it. She felt that he had lost a certain amount of freedom because of this, and worried that he would be bored going on holiday with just his parents.

Whilst many of these activities gave the young people something to do for a while, and presumably, gave their parents some sort of a break, not all led to the development of friendships. One mother said that although her son attended football club and 'normal' youth club twice a week, he didn't really have any proper friends there:

They're fine with him there, but he wouldn't get invited to someone's house for tea or something, no. That's one of the saddest things.

The issue of friendships was one that was prominent in most of the young people's interviews. There were two main aspects to this: one was the particular difficulty of leaving friends behind when the young people moved on from school or college; the second was the complicated issue of boyfriend/girlfriend relationships.

Few of the young people said that they had difficulty in making new friends, and this was borne out by many of their parents. Stuart said that he found it hard to make new friends, in his case because he didn't like talking to people that he didn't know; Bill hadn't made any friends at his new residential placement because of the age gap between him and the majority of the other residents. For most of the other youngsters, making friends was part of the normal routine of school, college or other daytime activities.

Although it was easy for most of the young people to make new friends, they understandably found it hard having to say goodbye to them when they moved on from school or college. Friends, for most of the young people, were made and maintained in the environment they were in at that time. Only a couple had kept in contact with school friends or friends from their home town if they had moved away. For the vast majority of the young people, the transition to adulthood was made more difficult than it otherwise might have been because of the repeated disruptions to their friendship networks. For Sarah, one of the hardest things about growing up had been losing her friends when she left school. She had made a number of very good friends at the college she currently attended, but was anxious that in a few months time when she was due to leave, she would have to say goodbye to this friendship group too. Julie said that starting somewhere new again was made even more difficult when she was constantly remembering and missing her old friends. Geoff had tears in his eyes when relating how he had lost touch with a friend from his school days when she had moved away to get a job after they had been through college together.

The second aspect of friendships that was prominent in many of the young people's interviews was the complicated issue of boyfriend/girlfriend relationships; an issue that was also commented on by a large proportion of their parents. Just over half (16 of the 27 young people interviewed) spoke about having a special boy- or girlfriend and many of them mentioned the difficulties of negotiating roles and boundaries within this friendship:

> *I used to have a few girlfriends when I was at college. But they did leave me. One was going out with another guy . . . I went out with her for about a year.*

Jake spoke about a girlfriend that he had just broken up with:

> *She wanted to get married and I had some doubts about it . . . Sometimes I can't sleep . . . me parents didn't want me to go out with her . . . 'cos she was far too disabled for me . . . so now I've accepted it.*

Geoff also described contemplating marriage and the difficult decision he had to make:

> *She said 'Will you marry me?' I was stunned, I was shocked. I didn't want to hurt a friendship . . . my girlfriend wanted to have sex as well. I didn't want to hurt any friendship at all . . . A choice between friendship or marriage. I took the friendship.*

Two of the young people mentioned attending a course to learn about relationships, which they had found useful. Others said that they had been taught about sex and relationships at school, or had had discussions about such things with their key workers or parents: 'I know a lot about it' said one young woman currently in a relationship, while another said:

> *I have got a boyfriend, but I don't have sex . . . Our team leader . . . had a word with me and my boyfriend about this* [i.e. relationships].

For some of the young people having a boy- or girlfriend was a sign of growing up: it gave them status and was a marker of moving towards adulthood. For others, however, it was something that they had yet to negotiate:

> *I don't really think it's the right thing yet . . . yeah . . . not yet.*

> *I would like to, but I need to think about it first.*

> *I used to have one . . . Do I want one? Umm . . . Yeah, I think I do.*

The views of parents about the relationships of their sons and daughters were quite mixed. Some didn't really like to entertain the possibility that a relationship could develop:

She's very vulnerable and very emotionally immature and can be easily persuaded . . . she's had a lot of boyfriend attention . . . And yes, she has had boyfriends, but not as we would think about it. It's a college thing and it's just friendliness within college . . . She's had boys coming to the house, which shocked the life out of us. She's had letters. We found little notes in her pocket . . . But so far, because we know where she is at a given time there's been no possibility of anything happening.

Others were more relaxed about the relationships of their son or daughter:

We did invite him to dinner and he's, I don't think he's right for Mary and I don't really think he thinks the world of Mary . . . but we're just letting it run its course and hopefully that will sort itself out.

Whether parents were accepting or otherwise of their son or daughter's relationships, many of them felt at a loss as to where to go for advice or support in talking through the issues involved:

I mean, you know, we thought we had problems when she was younger but this is getting out of our territory really. We really don't quite know how to handle it.

Talking to other parents in a similar situation was useful for some, but could also raise new issues to think through. Kath's mother said that as a result of meeting up with some parents from an Independent Living Group, she had been led into thinking about whether contraception might be an option for her daughter:

We hadn't done anything with Kath, and I kept thinking should I do something, should I not do something?

At the time of the interview, she was still undecided and was unsure where to go for further advice.

A couple of parents mentioned that they had spoken to social workers about their worries. As a result, one daughter had attended a 'young women's session' which her mother had felt was useful. Another mother, however, had been severely disappointed by her social worker's response and was left to deal with a distressing situation on her own as a single parent, backed up only by whatever 'sort of sex education I honestly don't know' that her son had received at school.

School was mentioned as a source of support by a couple of parents. For example, one mother had successfully persuaded her son's school to introduce sessions on personal and social education. She was keen for her son to be formally taught models of appropriate behaviour before he left school and moved on to other daytime activities.

The whole issue of leisure activities, friendships and relationships was problematic for many parents. More of them wanted more input in this area of transition planning than any other, and, it seems, parents were in need of the input as much, if not more than, their sons and daughters. Parents were doing their best to promote the personal and social development of their son or daughter through structured activities, often in difficult circumstances and without comprehensive knowledge of the options available. What was lacking for the young people was the opportunity for socialising informally with friends, while the need to sustain friendships was not given the consideration the young people felt it deserved. This is an important facet of transition planning that often seems to be overlooked. Young people need the opportunity to keep in contact with friends from different phases of their lives and to develop wider networks of peer relationships. Their parents need to be given the opportunity to explore for themselves, in a supportive environment, their thoughts and feelings about their sons or daughters developing friendships and relationships.

The move from paediatric health services to adult health services

A range of legislation sets out the duties of health agencies to provide services for young people during the transition period. The Code of Practice on the Identification and Assessment of Special Educational Needs (DfEE, 1994) expected that health services should be actively involved in the transition plan and that one of the questions addressed in the plan should be:

Does the young person have any special health or welfare needs which will require planning and support from health and social services now or in the future? (DfEE, 1994)

The Children Act 1989 states that joint planning and joint service arrangements are crucial for young disabled people in their transition to adulthood, and that this can only be effective if all relevant agencies and professionals are involved. The primary health care team is considered crucial to this. The Children Act also recognises the importance of maintaining good health, and that for disabled young people approaching adulthood, regular reviews are essential to prevent new problems occurring, or existing impairments deteriorating.

More recently, *Valuing People* (DoH, 2001) acknowledged that young disabled people may not be transferred from children's to adult services with adequate health care plans. It stresses the need for more effective links between children's and adult health services and identifies young people at transition as a priority group to receive a Health Action Plan as part of their person-centred plan, offered and reviewed at the time of transition from secondary education. The Health Action Plan should cover the need for health interventions, as well as health promotion issues.

The revised Special Educational Needs Code of Practice (DfES, 2001a) also advises a clear role for the involvement of health services in transition planning:

> *Health professionals involved in the management and care of the young person should provide advice towards transition plans in writing and, wherever possible, should attend the annual review meeting in Year 9. They should advise on the services that are likely to be required and should discuss arrangements for transfer to adult secondary health care services with the young person, their parents and their GP. (p. 142)*

It is generally recognised that the existing arrangements for the transition between children's and adult health services are not working well (Morris, 1999). This was borne out by the respondents to our survey. Over a half (52%) of the parents of those who had received some transition planning reported that the transfer to adult health services had not been dealt with *at all*. Fewer than a fifth (18%) thought that it had been covered well.[10]

We asked, in more detail, about the transfer to adult health services in our interviews with the parents and young people. In general, it was not a subject that was addressed in transition planning meetings, but one that had to be dealt with by the family as and when issues arose. There were two major aspects to this that parents found particularly distressing: first, the handover from children's to adult services itself; second the quality of service that the young people and their parents experienced within adult health provision.

The transition to adult health services was, on the whole, a rather abrupt affair. Only one parent mentioned a smooth transition while another said that

---

10. 17% of respondents thought that the transfer to adult health services had been 'partly' covered and 12% thought that any discussion of it was not applicable to them.

there had been some preparation for her son to move on from children's health services, although she described this as 'an ongoing saga'. For a third, an individual response to the service dilemma of where to place a sixteen-year-old young man with cardiac problems was being sought. The paediatric consultant had supported the local children's hospice in getting additional registration to be able to take the young man for short-term breaks up until the age of 25, as the adult hospice was not suitable for his particular needs.

For other families, however, the move to adult health services had been thrust upon them; typically, the young person and their parents were told at one visit that their next outpatient appointment or hospital admission would be with an adult team that they had not yet met.

The perceived gap in the quality and nature of health care that families met with within adult services was also very distressing. There were two issues here, the lack of continuity that families had received within paediatric services, and the lack of regular reviews. As Sarah's mother pointed out:

> *While Sarah was under the care of child services it was consistent, it was a very good consultant ... when we were handed over to adults ... every time we went we seemed to see a different person. And we'd spend half the appointment going over past history. The continuity had gone completely.*

Within children's health services the young people usually had regular appointments with health professionals. This gave their parents confidence that the young person's health needs were under regular review and any change in their condition would be picked up. When the young people moved in to adult health services, the onus was placed on the young person or their carer to contact the services if they had any problems. For one family, this had had a major impact on their daughter's health: the recommended annual check of her shunt had been inadvertently forgotten. Her parents felt that she was steadily deteriorating, possibly as a result of her shunt not working properly. They felt that attendance at a routine appointment might have highlighted the problem before it got to the point of affecting her life so severely.

The implications of the shift from regular, routine appointments to an 'as you need us' approach are immense; the latter approach assumes that there is someone able to pick up on signs that the young person is becoming unwell, if they cannot communicate this themselves. Yet this was not always the case as the young people were typically making transitions in other areas of their lives too at this stage, such as moving away from the family home to residential college or other provision. In these new environments they would be cared for or supported by people who were not always familiar with interpreting individual signs that the young person was becoming unwell.

This issue of trusting care staff to recognise signs of illness in their son or daughter was raised by a number of parents in a general way, and not just in connection with the transfer from children's to adult health services. They expressed concern that signs or symptoms might be missed, because the young person was unlikely to complain about being in pain, or because their behaviour changes were quite subtle when they were ill. For example, Stuart's mother recounted how she had explained to the care staff of the residential centre that he was attending that when he wasn't well he would become more quiet than usual and would isolate himself. When Stuart exhibited such behaviour, it was, however, misinterpreted, with the result that he developed severe, life-threatening bowel problems requiring a 10-week stay in hospital. His experiences at this time had a long-term psychological impact on him. His mother commented:

> The hard part was that we'd warned them that if he goes quiet, isolates himself, there's a problem and don't ignore it. But they did ignore it, that's what I found hard . . . he's moved on now but I do feel we're going to be in exactly the same position [in another residential care placement] because Stuart will deny if he's got a problem because now he's frightened of hospitals.

Even when care staff did pick up the signs or symptoms that a young person was showing, some parents felt that the staff didn't deal with health service professionals assertively enough on behalf of the young person or that health service professionals didn't listen to them well enough. This was a particular issue at transition time, when there was a tension between encouraging young people to be more independent and to speak up for themselves, whilst also ensuring their safety. One parent recalled how her son had broken his ankle but was unable to say where the pain was. He was x-rayed from thigh to shin but no fracture was found. The support workers with him recognised that it was probably his ankle that was painful, but did not insist on further x-rays and took him back to the residential school that he attended. The following day he was taken to a different hospital where another x-ray revealed his ankle was fractured.

A number of parents commented on the dismissive attitude of health professionals to their son or daughter. As Anna's mother said:

> Because she's got this mobility problem with one leg longer than the other, I've just forced the hospital to have a look at it . . . they weren't interested at all. I find the medical profession are not interested in Anna.

Sam's parents made similar comments:

> **Mother:** *The neurologist I saw . . . he wasn't interested at all. So he just said double the dose, or one and a half times the dose* [referring to her son's medication for epilepsy].
>
> **Father:** *Without even seeing him.*
>
> **Mother:** *Without doing anything.*
>
> **Interviewer:** *Not weighing him or checking anything?*
>
> **Mother:** *Nothing, nothing, he just sat there. He was eating a sandwich while we were sitting there. I was disgusted with the way he behaved.*

Another young man had been an inpatient in a psychiatric unit for six months for assumed mental health problems. When he was home for a weekend, his mother took him to their family GP for advice. The GP diagnosed an untreated thyroid problem in her son. Once appropriately treated for this, the young man improved and was soon discharged from hospital.

It is little wonder then that parents had concerns about whether their son or daughter would get appropriate medical attention as they progressed to adulthood. Not only did the parents have problems being listened to themselves at times, but they were also in the position of having to trust a different set of professionals that many of them had never met before. As one mother said:

> *We just passed over to another hospital, and you're just a number again.*

The move from children's social service teams to adult social services

A range of legislation sets out the duties of social service professionals to provide support for young people during the transition period. The Disabled Person's (Services, Consultation and Representation) Act 1986 requires that LEAs seek information from social service departments as to whether a child with a statement of educational need is disabled and may require services from the local authority when leaving school. The LEA must inform a designated social services officer of the date of the young person's first annual review after their 14th birthday, and must also inform the social services department between eight and 12 months before the young person's expected school leaving date.

Under the Children Act 1989 and the NHS and Community Care Act 1990, social services departments are required to arrange a multi-disciplinary assessment and provide care plans for children and adults with significant special needs.

The Code of Practice on the Identification and Assessment of Special Educational Needs (DfEE, 1994) states that where a young person has been looked after in a foster placement or a residential home or attended a residential school outside his or her own local authority, the LEA 'should seek to ensure liaison between all relevant LEAs and social services departments' (Para. 6:52) during the transition period.

More recently *Valuing People: A new strategy for learning disability for the 21st century* (DoH, 2001) acknowledges the lack of coordination between relevant agencies at transition and the need for effective links between children's and adult social services. It states that directors of social services are required to ensure that good links are in place between children's and adult services for people with learning difficulties as part of their new responsibility for quality under the Social Care Quality Framework.

The need for more effective links between children's and adult social services was borne out by our survey respondents. Over two-fifths (43%) of the parents of young people who had received some transition planning reported that the transfer to adult social services had not been dealt with *at all*, while only a quarter (26%) thought that it had been covered well.

We asked a number of open questions in the survey about transition, and some respondents took the opportunity to mention their particular experiences of social services teams. Almost a quarter (24%) of families who had received some transition planning said that the person who had helped *them* most through the transition planning process was their social worker, while 15% mentioned a social worker as the person who had helped the *young person* the most. We also asked about some of the most positive and negative things about transition for the young person and their parents. A handful of parents mentioned good relationships with a social worker as positive for them. Rather more mentioned that some of the most negative things about transition were: the late involvement of social services; their lack of input at transition planning meetings and beyond; their lack of commitment to the young person; the inconsistencies in dealing with different social workers and the lack of coordination between children's and adult social work teams. A number of parents had suggestions for change:

An efficient social worker might be helpful provided the social worker didn't change every year or so.

More cooperation and openness from social services.

Social services policy on transition.

The school cannot force social workers to come to reviews – perhaps they should be legally obliged to do so.

Social services should be more proactive.

We asked, in more detail, about the transfer to adult social services in our interviews with the parents and young people. For some families it had been a smooth transition, largely aided by key personnel who were consistent figures at planning meetings and who had got to know the young person well:

> *They appointed a transition manager . . . it was a new post that was generated I believe . . . because of problems in that area. And his sole remit is to look after the transition . . . he's been absolutely brilliant all the way through . . . he came to all the transition reviews from him taking up the post. And prior to that it was a bit bitty, I must say . . . She will probably* [be handed over to the adult team] *next year.*

> **Respondent:** *It's starting to happen now . . . They're doing work together . . . Although he won't come under adult social services until he's 18 I don't think, but they're starting –* [the adult social worker] *wants to come and meet him now and start talking to me.*

> **Interviewer:** *How many months of overlap will that be?*

> **Respondent:** *Nearly two years.*

For other families, the move from children's to adult social services teams was poor. Some parents highlighted a lack of continuity. One parent said that they had not received any prior warning that their social worker was changing:

> *They just wrote to me one day.*

Angie's family had had a particularly poor transition to adult social services; the social worker supporting her had left without handing over any information and with no replacement made. It had only come to light when no-one from social services had attended the planned review meeting and Angie's father had phoned the head of social services to complain. A pile of case notes was subsequently found on a desk that had belonged to the social worker, one of which was Angie's; none of them had been dealt with. In another case, the family were only informed about the impending move to adult social services when they asked about the continuation of short break services.

Others felt caught between two stools; the children's team had stopped their involvement, but the adult team wouldn't become involved until the young person reached a certain age – typically 18. A number of parents commented on the inflexibility of having an age entry for adult social service involvement and mentioned that an entry point that was more in keeping with the changes that were happening in the young person's life would be more appropriate. Tim's mother explained that her son had no social worker as he approached school-leaving because the social worker from the children's team had gone off on long-term sick and there was no replacement. As a result, they were left with no support until Tim was 18 when the adult division took over. Despite her circumstances, the adult division had told her:

We don't look at it 'til he's 18.

At this point his mother went through the complaints procedure where her complaint was upheld. She thought that there had been some improvement to this inflexible attitude for other youngsters since then.

Another issue that a number of parents commented on was the perceived gap in the quality and nature of support available to them within adult social services. Mary's mother explained how the transition to adult social services had happened for her daughter:

I think it was when she was 19 then she [the social worker from the children's team] *said 'I won't be coming anymore and I doubt very much if you'll see much of the people who are taking over from me'. That's what the social worker said to me . . . And I saw her once this lady* [the social worker from the adult team]. *And then I got a letter from her to say that she'd left and that if I had any difficulties I was to contact the team at X . . . but she* [Mary] *hadn't been allocated to anybody specifically.*

For some of the families the lack of consistency in who they saw was a particular problem:

It always seems to be there's a name and there's a number and everybody changes unbelievably.

We haven't got a social worker [now]. *We did have one who came and sorted something out and then it got changed.*

In general, there was more dissatisfaction overall with social services than satisfaction. In contravention of the guidance, social workers did *not* appear to be regular attendees at transition planning meetings, nor fully engaged as members of a multi-disciplinary team. Those parents who reported the most favourable experiences of transition to adult social work teams were those who had worked with their new social workers as a lead-up to the transfer, or who had been supported by a nominated transition worker during the process.

Conclusion

This chapter gives ample evidence of the range of complex issues that parents are dealing with whilst their son or daughter with learning difficulties moves beyond school. Typically, parents of young adults are making their own transition into a phase where they should be freer of the responsibilities associated with having a younger, more dependent family. However, for some of the families in our study, parents had less independence from their youngsters as they approached adulthood, than when they were still at school. As the youngsters moved into adult services there was less short-break provision available, fewer social opportunities for them, less than 'full-time' day opportunities and unpredictable services that might be cancelled or curtailed at short notice. A universal entitlement to full-time education was replaced by restricted options dependent on local circumstances and, it seems, luck. As a result, it was less easy for parents to plan their days and envisage their own futures than when their youngsters were at school. Abigail's father described his daughter's leaving school as having 'a rug pulled out from us'; he had been forced to give up work to support Abigail during the times that she wasn't at college, and her short-break provision had stopped. Both parents felt that things had become more restrictive for them, Abigail and her sister. As her father explained:

> *It's not so much . . . I don't need a career, now, at this age, but it's just not having the choice at all . . . we're thinking now that this could be our whole life.*

Sam's father commented:

> *It felt as though it was going to be easy, and now it's become incredibly difficult . . . it's just this stone wall.*

The needs of parent carers are further considered in Chapter 6.

Chapter 4: Transitions to adulthood: what makes a difference?

Young people's experiences of the transition to adulthood are helped (or hindered) by factors that are more connected to the environment and context in which transition occurs, than on the actual transition process itself.

This chapter focuses on family circumstances and three other issues that our study highlighted as having an impact on moves towards independence: concerns about safety and risk, financial matters and anxieties about using public transport.

Family circumstances

Families provide an important context for children and young people with regards to their attitudes towards education and employment, facilitating their moves towards independence, giving information about sex and relationships, and providing financial and practical support to maintain leisure and social activities (Morrow & Richards, 1996). Both emotionally and practically, families are an important source of support for most young people, even though adolescence is typically a time when young people pull away from their parents and begin to assert their own independence.

Our questionnaire did not ask how families felt about the resources that they had to cope with the impact of their childrens' disability or the systems involved. However, a number of parents did comment in writing about this:

> *We are articulate, well-off parents who know how to obtain information and 'get what we want' – we are fortunate. However, for the average person with lack of funds things would have been very different and in similar circumstances our daughter would not have ended up in the school/college of our choice.*

> *The reason where we are, I think, with Emma, is unfortunately, he who makes their opinions and wants and needs most known gets what they want. There are millions of parents out there who don't have the ability a) to do that or b) to be sorted on the network.*

Emotional resources (like financial ones) are of great significance in affecting the degree of support a family is able to give their young person. Emotional issues often come to the fore at transition; both when expected transitions do occur, for example when a young person leaves home, and also when expected transitions do not occur (and consequently parents may be seen as over-protective or unable to 'let go'). One mother explained her own feelings when her son had visited home after recently moving away:

He didn't want to go back. I didn't want him to go back . . . but he had to go back. I had to let him go back because I would have kept him at home. I would have been over-protective.

Many of the parents we interviewed spoke about the emotional side of relationships in the family at transition:

She's 21 and she's straining at the leash in a way, but doesn't know how to sort of go about it. And it's ever so difficult to, I mean I enjoy doing things with her, but on the other hand it means that I'm not doing things that I ought to be doing with my husband, you know.

Some parents spoke of the difficulties siblings faced:

And really, sort of over the past few years, her teenage years, she's really struggled with having Abigail as a sister . . . it's built up over the years. She's always had this view that we give Abigail a lot more than we give her, and that Abigail gets a lot more. And there are times that's so angered me. But it's so difficult as a parent to deal with . . . for instance if we used to go out, people would say . . . If I was with Suzanne, and people say to me 'Oh how's your daughter getting along?' And there's little Suzanne here. And I would actually, purposefully say 'Oh which daughter do you mean?' And it would sound, probably, horrible to the other person, but I was doing it to try and protect Suzanne. But in a way you can't because that is a very strong message that the daughter that matters is the one they're asking about . . . One thing I was absolutely taken aback by – one day, I was having a heart to heart with her, and sort of saying, you know, 'We can't do anything to change the situation. And you know, I'm not quite sure about the situation that you find so difficult. You know? Explain it to me'. She said, 'Well, for one thing, I'll never have any nieces and nephews will I? I'll never be an aunty' . . . I was taken totally by surprise . . . I couldn't believe it! . . . I just hadn't thought of that at all.

There is evidence that siblings contribute to the care of children with learning difficulties (Swain and Thirlaway, 1994) but it seemed that as the young people in our study moved towards adulthood, parents were keen to protect their other children from the expectation that they should help with day-to-day care at home. Nonetheless, a number of parents were clearly relieved that there were other family members who could support the young person if anything happened to themselves in the future.

Well, hopefully, my daughter will always be there. I mean, I don't know where in the country she'll be, but I'm sure she'll always make sure Tim is OK.

I think it's fair to say his two sisters will look out for him.

Most families experience the usual ups and downs of day-to-day living. In some families, however, more major changes might take place affecting the amount of emotional or practical support available. For example, over half (55%) of the families answering the questionnaire, who had a young person who had left school, said one or more major events had happened in their son or daughter's life as they moved towards adulthood. The events most commonly reported were the death of a close family member, siblings leaving home, parental divorce or family reconstitution and parental illness. Many of these families (about two-thirds) reported that such events had greatly affected the young person and their progress through transition to adulthood:

My husband left us when Zoe had been at college for six months. This was very traumatic for her . . . she withdrew into herself and wouldn't talk about it.

Divorce. Still unable to accept the fact. Considerable difficulty with accepting step-mother. Very upset and continues to revisit problems.

On the other hand, other young people (about a third) were said to have coped well with major family changes, and to have matured as a result:

Joe has attended four funerals in the family. He coped very well and was most supportive to me and his mother.

I got divorced from my wife three years before [when he was 15]. *With hindsight I still cannot detect any particular difficulty.*

Some had been pushed through the transition process sooner than might have happened otherwise:

The start really coincided with the quite sudden death of my wife, which in some ways forced me into things perhaps. And it's then when I started getting in touch with the headmaster about transition and careers advice and he was involved. And it was only by making appointments to see them earlier than would have happened that I was able to get my hands on various leaflets and pamphlets.

There were no clear predictors of what might have led some young people to cope better than others in relation to the following variables: their age, sex or ethnicity, whether they lived at home; had had any transition planning; were still in their first placement after leaving school; or whether the professionals supporting them at the time of the major family change took it into account in a helpful way when planning their transition towards adulthood.

In our interviews with the young people and their parents, we tried to explore whether there were any particular aspects of family life, or things that the family could do, which eased the transition of young people towards adulthood.

A few of the young people that we spoke to had thoughts about this. Some who lived away from home spoke about the importance of contact with their families, through visits, telephone contact or by the presence of photographs or mementos. Others spoke of the encouragement their parents gave them:

She's always helping me to live my life.

I didn't have any social workers in my life . . . We just stay as a family like. My parents supported me all the time.

My parents . . . very supporting and I trust them.

For other young people, it was a sense of a place in the family, and of being able to offer something themselves, that seemed to give them satisfaction and a sense of moving towards adulthood. Jake spoke of how he supported his elderly grandmother:

She gets a bit down and I have to comfort her sometimes . . . me grandma's getting a bit senile . . . On Wednesdays I go and see her.

Adam spoke of helping his brother on a job, and others mentioned helping around the house:

I'll hoover up and dust and make teas, cups of teas.

Most parents that we spoke to felt that supporting their son or daughter through transition was a balancing act. On the one hand they were promoting the young person's independence, and on the other trying to do the best they could given other pressures and concerns of day-to-day family life. As two mothers explained:

You know, people will ask her a question and I'll answer it before I've even thought of it. And it's terrible. It's so unfair on her . . .

I think we've made a mistake in doing too much for her, only because usually we're in a rush and it's easier and quicker for you to do it.

A number of parents commented on how they had used the experiences of their other children to guide the way for the young person with learning disabilities:

I am expecting her to have employment. If she doesn't I will force her in some. If I have to hold her hand and go I will. I want her to have a proper job . . . I had a similar thing when my son left school, although he wasn't special needs. 'There's no jobs. Your son isn't top of the class. We'll teach him how to fill the dole forms in'. That's from the Careers Officer. I went absolutely mad and said 'Don't you dare'. Now he is a businessman . . . he is affluent. He is well away and I thought to myself this is the lad who they were going to show the dole forms to. So I'm not taking that off anyone again . . . Yes I want the employment. I want her to have a job. I want her to go out in the morning feeling she is worth something. Even if I have to pay the wages or whatever, I am going to make sure that she does it.

As siblings moved on to college, away from home or into employment, they would be used as an example for the young person with learning difficulties. For example, one mother talked about how she went out shopping 'for college' with the young person with learning difficulties in the same way as she had with her other children. Other parents said that they also introduced the idea of going to college in this way:

He's coped very well with it. I think, in a way, it's because [his sister] *has gone from school to school to university. And, you know, we've sort of said . . . like* [his sister] *he's going . . . away to school.*

He had brothers and sisters who went off to do the next bit of learning so it was a natural expectation.

Thus there were a number of strategies that parents were using to guide and support their children through towards adulthood. For many, it was a case of trial and error, coping with each change as it arose. For others, there was some degree of planning and control, but even then, most families found the transition of their child with learning difficulties an emotionally difficult time, more so than the transition of any of their other children. Overwhelmingly, it seemed to be the lack of support for the families that was common to all. As one mother eloquently put it:

No, no. Mothers don't have needs do they!

Circumstances inhibiting the young people's moves towards independence

There were a number of circumstances that seemed to generally inhibit young people's moves towards independence. These were, on the whole, not age-related factors but were often exacerbated at transition, a time when young people generally are testing the waters of independence.

'Independence' is a concept that often gives rise to confusion and is open to different interpretations. By 'independence' we do not mean doing everything for oneself. Rather, independence is about having choice and control over decisions in one's life, with appropriate support, including technical support, to participate fully in the life of the community. Mary provided a good illustration of this interpretation of independence. She found it difficult to manage crossing the road safely, but to get to her day centre by the public bus service she had to cross a very busy main road. The solution for her was to use a mobile phone. When she arrived at the bus stop opposite the day centre she would phone the staff and someone would come and help her cross the road. In this way, Mary was maintaining her independence travelling by public transport and the support she needed in crossing the road was under her control.

The key concerns that seemed to inhibit the young people's moves towards more independent living fell into three categories: safety and risk; financial (largely social security benefits) issues; and the use of public transport.

Safety and risk

We did not ask the parents that we interviewed directly about their fears concerning the personal safety of the young person, but 13 of the 27 parents we spoke with spontaneously mentioned their concerns in this area. For seven (a quarter) of the young people, serious incidents threatening their personal safety had occurred, ranging from severe bullying to serious sexual assault and rape.

And he had to overcome bullying because there was bullying going on in the college and the trouble with Nick is . . . he may fib and exaggerate but he doesn't lie and the times when he has said things to me and I have said 'That can't be true' and he came home once from college and said this boy held a knife to his throat and you think that can't be true and I actually phoned the college up and it had been true and he had been threatened.

In this instance his mother felt that the college had been supportive to Nick, and his assailant was suspended, but other parents reported cases where serious instances were ignored:

He was being sexually abused by another pupil . . . he'd told the care staff, he'd told the teacher. And when I rang – several times I rang – they said, 'Oh, there's nothing sexual going on'. So I even spoke to a policewoman, off the record, and said 'Would you say this was sexual abuse?' 'Oh definitely' she said 'Do you want us to investigate?' I said no . . . they didn't believe us because the headmaster and all the staff were covering up 'Nothing going on, nothing going on'.

She got really really badly bullied. And I started to, I tried to talk to them about it and sort it out. I even, in the end, had to go right up to the top of the LEA. And I couldn't get anywhere . . . they started to say she was self-harming which she wasn't. You can't hit yourself across the back with a cricket bat. You know, you can't damage your kidneys yourself.

We are unaware of the outcome of all of the serious incidents that had occurred, but it seemed that action was rarely taken against the perpetrators involved. Both of the young people mentioned above were withdrawn from school as a result of their experiences, and both experienced long periods at home (17 months in one case and two years in the other) before they were offered a place at another school. Another mother recalled what happened after her daughter was seriously sexually assaulted:

She phoned us . . . I rang the police and the police were here when she arrived . . . and they handled it extremely well . . . they were very very supportive but they didn't end up convicting . . . they didn't convict because they needed Mary to give evidence in court. And we weren't prepared for her to live through it again in court. Originally they said she could do video evidence, but because she was over 18 . . . she was expected to be there and we didn't want her . . . he still carried on going to the college . . . she had to cope with that . . . we went to see the Principal obviously at the college and profuse apologies and everything like this, and they said 'Oh yes, he's getting some help'.

This young woman remained in the college for a further six months, until the end of her course, despite the fact that her assailant was a fellow student.

It is not surprising, therefore, that so many of the parents we interviewed were particularly concerned about the safety of their children. We do not know how many of the young people whose parents responded to our questionnaires had similar experiences. What we do know, is that of all respondents in our interview sample – selected on criteria other than to do with issues of personal safety – a quarter reported that their children had suffered a serious incident of one sort or another. A further quarter, without prompting, also mentioned particular concerns about their safety:

> *It's a risk. You've not got a second chance have you? . . . she's very very naive and trusting and I suppose we're over-protective in some ways but you can't always get two chances.*

In our interviews with the young people we asked them directly whether they had experienced being bullied or laughed at, in the context of the worst things to deal with whilst growing up. For 18 of the 27 young people that we interviewed (67%) bullying or physical assault was, or had been, an issue. Most of the young people were quite clear about what they meant by the term bullying and mentioned things such as being 'tormented', 'picked on', 'put down' or 'spat at'. Gestures such as fighting or laughing at someone were pointed at by non-verbal young people. One young woman said: 'I don't mind being laughed at but I don't like being bullied' while one of the young men said:

> *The worst thing in my life is getting picked on ... because of my Down's Syndrome.*

Five of the seven young people whose parents talked about serious incidents against them mentioned those incidents spontaneously when asked about bullying, while a sixth said 'That's me, look' whilst pointing to an illustration of bullying in the *Growing Up* booklet, and then signed the Makaton for 'sad'.

Discussing such a sensitive issue with the young people was difficult for a number of reasons. First, the discussions came largely out of the blue. Although we asked the youngsters about bullying, we did not expect to hear such horrific stories of assault or abuse. Only one parent had forewarned us about the incident and told us that her daughter had said that she did not want to talk about it, which we respected. All of the other incidents were recounted to us during the course of the interviews themselves, without the interviewers having any prior knowledge of them. Second, we were interviewing the young people for an hour or two and would then leave, and did not want to run the risk of stirring up potentially disturbing memories. So we did not question the young people in any depth about their experiences, just verified what they were saying and moved the conversation on appropriately. One such conversation went as followed:

> **Young person:** *I've been hit by a cricket bat . . . and things like that.*
>
> **Interviewer:** *Oh dear . . . that sounds as though it was a horrible thing for you.*
>
> **Young person:** *Yes it was. It was traumatic actually.*
>
> **Interviewer:** *Were you able to tell anybody about that, and get any help with that?*
>
> **Young person:** *No, I didn't get no help. It was only when Mum saw the bruises . . . Yeah, she's got photos of that, somewhere.*
>
> **Interviewer:** *Right. And did she tell the teachers at school, then? You're shaking your head. No. OK. It can be upsetting. Shall we talk about something else?*

Serious incidents, such as those mentioned by the parents and young people, frequently leave a legacy of fear and anxiety in both those who have experienced them, and those close to them. It was of little surprise, therefore, that the young people with whom we spoke, who had gone through such experiences, expressed anxieties about aspects of personal safety or difficulties in standing up for themselves:

> *I don't like it if my room's full of darkness – it scares me. That's why I always have my light on every night. I can't sleep in the dark.*

> *I just feel a bit scary . . . I just feel closed inside.*

It was also quite commonplace for the other young people that we interviewed to mention aspects of personal safety in the concerns that they had about growing up. For some of the young people, these concerns centred on road safety and being anxious about crossing the road:

> *They've shown me how to cross the road and I've done it once or twice on my own but I still don't feel safe . . . Like if they tell me to cross this road to go down to the shop, I reckon I would still be there an hour later when they got back. I don't cross the road unless I'm safe. I'm a bit wary of the traffic . . . If there were no roads I'd go out.*

For others, safety from certain other people was their main concern:

> *I want to know there's people about . . . In case someone came to me and have a go at you.*

> *In case someone gets me.*

> *I found it very scary . . . like the local – or something are just going to abuse you or something, or kill you or something.*

> *When I'm out there I am in danger, I am in danger of strangers walking past.*

The overwhelming impression that we got from the interviews with the young people with learning difficulties and their parents was that fear and anxiety about personal safety was hampering the young people in their moves towards adulthood. In many cases these fears were, sadly, justified, given the stories of assault or bullying that we were told. In other cases, parents recognised that they might be being 'over-protective', especially when they compared the young person with their siblings, but considered the young person to be vulnerable and at risk. It was a dilemma that many parents and young people faced with little or no support.

Financial matters

This was the second of the general issues that seemed to inhibit the young people's moves towards independence. Financial resources are a key factor in young people's participation in a range of social and other activities that form an important part of becoming an independent adult. Young people are often in a contradictory position; they may be forced into prolonged economic dependence on their families, whilst simultaneously being drawn into consumer markets. In general, research suggests that participation in consumer markets is important to people's sense of 'who they are' in the construction of individual identity, differentiated from one's family of origin (Morrow and Richards, 1996).

Young disabled people reaching the age of 16 may be entitled, for the first time, to various social security benefits paid on the grounds of disability. In the questionnaires, we asked parents about whether claiming, or changing, benefits should have been, or was, covered in transition planning. For those who reported that there had been no transition planning for their son or daughter this was seen as an important issue, with almost three-quarters (73%) of parents saying that they thought claiming or changing benefits should have been covered. Yet this was not the experience of the majority of young people who had received transition planning. For over half (54%) of the young people who had received transition planning and since left school, claiming or changing benefits was not covered at all. Another 22% of parents thought that it was only covered 'partly'.

We followed up this issue in the interviews with parents. For many of them, claiming the correct benefits for the young person had been fraught with confusion:

> *It was like* [being] *in the middle of a maze . . . You're going round and round and back.*

> *I never discussed benefits with anybody.*

> *I know I never claimed the Income Support because I didn't know I could until I claimed something else.*

Not only were parents not given relevant information, but some were also given misinformation, as one parent explained:

> *We had a guy come round from the Benefits Office . . . he made an appointment . . . this was with regard to proving that Stuart existed because he's now an adult in his own right we had to prove Stuart existed . . . I said is there now anything we need to change with the fact he's now 16? He said, 'Not as far as I'm aware . . .' It wasn't until he actually started at* [college]. *He was 16 in February. He started at college in September and . . . we suddenly realised Stuart should have been on other benefits, nobody told us about it and we couldn't get it backdated, it was just horrendous. Nobody tells you anything to do with the benefits system.*

Very few of the parents had been given good information about claiming benefits at transition. Information came from a variety of sources: information days at school or college; benefits promotional events unconnected with school or college; organisations for disabled people or carers; or just by chance:

> *The school had got a woman from social services – no, from the Benefits Office . . . she came to the school. It was something to do with a woman who was on secondment to do this; to offer schools this service . . . And this woman gave a talk one evening, just a broad overview, and then she said, you know, 'If any of you want to come and see me then I will help you apply for the Severe Disability', and I went and saw her. She told me exactly what to do, at what age, so that was excellent.*

We weren't informed she stopped child allowance and went on to Income Support. We didn't know . . . I think there was a bus over at [nearest town]. We get, like, buses coming round . . . and I think my husband popped in there about something else – another benefit. And they were actually so helpful. And they told him that she should be on Income Support. 'Weren't you told?' And he said 'No'. So they gave him the form and said 'Fill it in'.

It was just by chance I happened to be reading the Benefit book.

Access to money and learning how to budget appropriately are important aspects of the transition to adulthood. Yet few of the young people that we interviewed managed their own money. Some parents said that the young person was 'baffled' by money, that they 'hadn't got a clue' or 'couldn't handle it', couldn't recognise its worth or might be vulnerable to exploitation. Just two of the young people mentioned that they used their own bank account. Others spoke of allowances, pocket money or of having to ask someone in order to be able to buy something.

Nine of the young people that we spoke to claimed that they had no problems with handling their money when they had access to it. Most were able to say what they spent their money on – items such as sweets or crisps, lunches, books, magazines or music. A few paid a contribution to their living expenses at home, to holidays or towards buying their own clothes.

Another nine young people said that they had difficulties with their money. They reported a number of problems, such as keeping their money safe, giving or receiving the right amount, or having enough:

Ah money – I can sort it out all right. It's just when I go to buy things I don't get it right.

I always worry about money . . . the big money.

I do worry about money. I don't worry about how much I've got. I worry about if I've got enough.

Parents figured prominently in the allocation of money to the young people we interviewed. This was irrespective of their age or gender. A number of comments suggested that this was an aspect of gaining more independence that was being worked on. Parents spoke of trying to teach their sons or daughters about money themselves, or that the youngsters were learning this at school or college. Some youngsters had their money portioned out into daily amounts to help them with this.

We met three young people who were in paid employment. They had significantly more control over their use of money than any of the other young people. It was clear, nevertheless, that their parents kept a watchful eye on things. Being able to buy into the adult world outside of their jobs gave these young people additional status. One lent his brother some money, two paid contributions to their family for their 'keep'. For all of them, earning their own money was important for their self-identity.

Young people who were entitled to social security benefits in their own right seemed not to feel this way. Perhaps it was that their benefits were merged into the household income and were not specifically targeted at the individual. Perhaps it was that this 'substitute' rather than real wage hampers the move towards adult status. We asked the young people what it was that they felt would make them feel 'grown up'. One of the most frequent responses was 'a job'. This was alongside responses to do with chronological age or the passing of birthdays, getting married and moving away from home. For many of these young people getting a job, and thus having money that they earned themselves, was *the* marker of adulthood – a marker that would remain, all too often, merely an aspiration.

Public transport

The opportunities of many young people are limited by the availability of transport to get them to the places that they want to go. This is even more the case for disabled young people, for whom lack of transport can have a significant impact on their opportunities for leisure activities and making and maintaining friendships (Morris, 1999).

Of the young people who had left school having had some transition planning, only a third (34%) of respondents said that transport arrangements for any post-school provision had been dealt with well. Only 13% of those still at school had discussed transport, presumably reflecting the fact that such arrangements can only be made once specific post-school provision had been agreed. Almost three-quarters (74%) of parents with a young person still at school thought that information about transport arrangements to any post-school provision should be covered in the transition plan.

Transport is clearly an issue for young disabled people generally, not just in relation to post-school provision. Young people need access to social and leisure activities at times and in places convenient to them. They do not always want to be reliant on parents to take and collect them from events since this can constrain their activities. Catching the bus home alone, or having one's own independent travel arrangements is a rite of passage for many young people. One mother explained her feelings when her daughter had reached this stage:

One day I – well, she hadn't been at college long, had she?. No, about four weeks. And I said to [husband] 'Oh, I know, we'll get the shopping done early and we'll go and pick her up and give her a lift back'. We chased all round and I met her at the bus stop. 'Oh, Sue, we're going to give you a lift home'. 'Umm . . .' she said. And I was crushed, totally crushed. She said 'No, I want to go home on the bus' . . . I said 'All right'. So we had to come home without her. We couldn't believe it that she'd want to . . . sit on the bus, the creaky old bus for an hour.

It seemed, from the interviews with parents and young people, that transport was an issue for both. For the parents, there was a general sense of fear in letting the young people travel independently. This was either because parents did not believe that they could manage it, or because they were worried about their physical safety:

I mean, if you stood her at the bus stop and she got on, unless somebody actually said 'Get off' I don't think – and also, she'd get too worried about it. You know, the agitation would be too much.

The social worker said to me, 'Isn't Andrew capable of going and coming?' I said, 'Well, I think he probably could, but I don't want him standing down there [waiting for a bus] because if anybody picked him up in the morning, I wouldn't know he was missing 'til it was time for him to come home'. And you don't know, do you? There's some funny people about.

For the young people, it seemed that transport was an issue because of its unpredictability:

I got left behind twice at college and I get worried about that . . . my transport hasn't come . . . I had to ring them up and say 'Where are you?'

I don't know what times they [the buses] are, you see . . . Sometimes they're a bit late or something.

One young man spoke of his wish to use the bus:

I'd like to learn to use the bus, yes.

While a number said that they would like to learn how to drive:

Things that I would like to do but I can't . . . like drive a car . . . people who I was at college with they drive a car but I don't so that's not fair.

Where transport arrangements were working well, they supported the young person's move to independence. Parents noted that their children had gained more confidence or become more flexible when they had managed their transport arrangements independently of their parents. Some spoke of ways that the transition to more independent travelling arrangements had been handled. In general, what seemed to work best for the young people had been a very gradual introduction with plenty of support. So, for example, one mother explained how an occupational therapist (OT) had first taken her daughter to see the bus station nearest college in the car. Then the OT and her daughter did the journey together, and when they were happy with that, the OT would put her daughter on the bus at one end and drive round to meet her at the bus stop where she would get off. By introducing this gradually, her daughter was said to cope very well with the long bus journey to college and back. This arrangement had been facilitated through a Community Care Assessment, and was an example of particular action taken to support the young person at transition. Another strategy that some of the young people used was to carry, and use, a mobile phone should they miss their transport or it not turn up.

Summary

The last two chapters have highlighted a number of key transition processes that generally signify the move to full adult status. They have also emphasised some very real problems that some young people have in their move towards adult status:

- The lack of choice about what sort of future provision the young people would move on to, especially after leaving college

- The lack of easily accessible, comprehensive information available for parents and young people about what some of the future possibilities *might* be

- The significant degree of unhappiness and stress experienced by many parents in seeking appropriate options for their son or daughter

- Whether or not a youngster had transition planning did not appear to make much difference to the outcomes of the young people (with regards to employment status or moving into their own home). Indeed, it rather seemed to be down to 'luck'

- Very few options other than some form of residential provision for most young people when considering leaving home

- A lack of information about leisure and social activities, even though families overwhelmingly wanted this to be covered in transition planning

- Repeated disruptions to the young people's friendship networks

- No matter how accepting or otherwise parents were about their son or daughter's developing sexual relationships, many of them felt at a loss as to where to go for advice or support in talking through the issues

- The lack of attention paid to the transfer to adult health services in transition planning meetings (so that the family had to address this issue as and when the need arose)

- A lack of coordination between children's and adult social work teams, inconsistencies in dealing with different social workers, and the lack of social services' input at transition planning meetings and beyond

- A perceived gap in the quality and nature of care that young people and their parents found within adult health *and* social services

- Key factors holding back the young people from developing their independence were: concerns about safety and risk; financial (largely social security benefits) issues; and anxieties about the use of public transport

- Out of a sample of all respondents in the survey, selected on criteria other than to do with issues of personal safety, a quarter of young people had suffered a serious incident of one sort or another

- For many parents, claiming the correct social security benefits for the young person had been fraught with confusion

- Parents figured prominently in the allocation of money to the young people, irrespective of the young person's age or gender, other than where the young person was in paid employment

- Using public transport was an issue for parents because of their fear of letting the young person travel independently. It was an issue for the young people because of its unpredictability.

Chapter 5: What makes for a better transition experience?

Valuing People (DoH, 2001) states the Government's expectation, that people with learning difficulties and their carers will be fully involved in planning, monitoring, reviewing and evaluating the quality of the services they receive. Service providers need a clear picture of the experience of those receiving services, and feedback from them about what might help make services better. Throughout this project we have been concerned not only with what happens at transition 'on the ground' but also with what helps make transition experiences good. We inquired about this in the postal survey, by asking about the most positive aspects of the transition planning process for the young person and their parents, as well as inviting respondents to describe any changes they would like to see. The interviews enabled us to follow up and discuss further any comments or ideas about good quality transition experiences. Some ideas about what makes transition experiences better have been mentioned in previous chapters. In this chapter, we bring them, and others, together to discuss the key ingredients of a better transition experience.

The young people's perspective

About half of those parents who had experienced planning described what they felt had been the most positive aspects of the process for their son or daughter. One group of 'positive factors' was directly related to activities affecting the young person at transition. About a third (30%) of responses referred to work experience or link placements that provided fresh experiences, a sense of the next step, a time to accommodate to new locations and a way to inform choices. Many of the young people themselves also said that they had enjoyed visits to future options to see for themselves what they might be like and to get more of a sense of what they would be moving on to. Important points in making this a positive experience were: the gradual move to the new environment over a period of time with plenty of support; being accompanied by one's friends or having someone familiar there when they arrived; and the availability of someone to talk to about the new environment, both in advance and after any visits.

Approximately 10% of parents thought that their son or daughter's involvement in planning was the most positive aspect of the process for the young person. Even if the young person was not participating actively, it mattered that they were included at meetings or in discussions elsewhere, that they were given choices and had chances to state preferences. Again, this was highlighted in the interviews with the young people. Some mentioned seeing videos or brochures about possible options and choosing which to visit; others appreciated information days at school or college, talking about the future with their teachers or friends and being able to make choices for themselves.

Emotional preparation was also mentioned as a positive aspect of the transition planning process for the young people. Thirteen per cent of parents said that starting to plan early had allowed enough time for incremental steps, ensuring a gradual transition with 'no surprises'. Some said that drawing a parallel between the young people with learning difficulties moving on from school and their siblings moving away to university or on to work had been helpful. Practices that were to do with marking progression in terms of an altered post–16 curriculum (with or without moving to different premises), building independent living skills, self-esteem and social skills were also seen as positive in helping the young people prepare emotionally for leaving school.

Another group of responses focused on professional practice. There were a number of aspects to this. Parents commented on staff commitment to consider fully (and provide evidence of) support needs, talents, wishes and interests of the young person. This was key to knowing what sort of provision to seek for the youngsters. Bill's mother, for example said:

> Bill's teacher … made sure that … Bill had a book of all his achievements, and you know, videos of trips they'd been on, holidays … that was all up-to-date and together … his yearly reports … the college had all that to go with him.

Some parents gave examples of staff being particularly flexible, such as school personnel visiting future options with the young person or prospective staff visiting current provision to help plan support, as being the most positive aspects of transition for the young person.

Information was also key to positive experiences for the youngsters. Schools, careers advisers, colleges and social workers were acknowledged as being especially helpful to the young person through providing knowledge about procedures and suitable provision. Professional input at multi-agency meetings, where information could be shared between those who knew the young person well and those who would be negotiating with decision makers, was also highly valued.

The parents' perspective

Almost a quarter (21%) of parents who gave information about the most positive aspects of the transition process for themselves highlighted the experience of being actively involved as being the most positive feature. Parents valued being listened to, feeling their views had been heard, participating in discussions about future opportunities for their son or daughter, being kept informed or actually 'driving' the process. A further 15% mentioned that they appreciated being 'backed up' or supported by the school, especially in helping to secure the future provision of their (and their youngster's) choice.

Professionals' input accounted for another cluster of responses. Some parents thought that the most positive aspects of the transition process for them had been having confidence in school or future care staff who showed dedication, had their son or daughter's best interests at heart or worked in a helpful and thorough way. Staff support and encouragement was valued when it enabled parents themselves to be involved, come to terms with likely future needs, 'persevere' with what seemed right and so do their best to achieve a satisfactory post-school transition for their son or daughter. Other parents mentioned the contribution of non-school staff (careers, social workers, benefits advisers and college) as especially valuable, and the help of transition coordinators or multi-agency approaches.

About 10% of parents mentioned that one of the most positive things about transition for them was the 'observation of progress' as their son or daughter gained new friends, skills and confidence, got access to 'a college experience' and generally became more capable. Other parents similarly noted the satisfaction of 'seeing a future' for their youngster. Parents also mentioned the good provision of information from other parents, careers advisers, school staff and (on one occasion) previous pupils; support from other parents; an early start to transition planning so allowing a variety of options to be explored; and there being a choice of provision available to choose from.

What changes would parents like to the transition planning process?

Two-thirds of parents who had experience of transition planning said that they would like to see changes to the process. On average, each of these suggested two improvements. A lot of the changes recommended by parents were *exactly* what statutory guidance says should routinely happen. Furthermore, a large proportion were what would normally constitute good practice according to published guidance. Clearly, for many of the families in our survey, statutory guidance was not being followed as it should have been.

Parents recommended changes along lines that statutory guidance says should be routine:

- schools should initiate transition planning reviews at the prescribed time

- efforts should be made to inform and involve the young person

- review meetings should be a priority for professionals so that all key people are present to plan jointly and be able to consider all of the options

- a structured plan, with actions ascribed to named individuals should result from each review meeting

- there should be regular review meetings and discussions to revisit and update the transition plan.

Changes recommended by parents that would normally constitute good practice according to published guidance:

- supporting young people through transition with an independent advocate

- parents and young people being supported through transition by social services staff who are informed, efficient, competent, constant, proactive, and liaise well between children's and adult services

- transparency throughout the whole transition process, so that young people and their parents know what to expect and when, and so that there is clear accountability for actions

- good, effective communication at all levels and between everyone (including agencies) involved in transition, so that information gets to those who need it

- enabling families to get the knowledge they need to support their young person into adulthood

- supplying parents and young people with factually correct information in a range of formats

- the existence of a range of inclusive options for young people to choose from, that they and their parents are supported to find out about, visit and apply to

- the provision of a structured programme of activities for young people in their last 18 months at school which would link in to their next placement, whether college, work placements or other daytime activities

- the early confirmation of funding for placements.

A few parents suggested additional changes not currently part of statutory guidance. Many were creative responses to the difficulties that these families had experienced themselves. Others were 'wish lists' of things that the families thought might have made their own experiences better. Each was valid feedback to service providers about what might help improve transition.

The first set of suggestions focused on better preparations for transition planning meetings. Parents mentioned that it would be helpful to have more advice and guidance on how to prepare for transition planning meetings, the key people attending and their duties and obligations, the expected involvement of parents and young people, and how to make sure the meetings are effective. This could all be provided at an initial meeting to brief parents and young people before the 14+ transition plan meeting:

> *I would like to have had an initial meeting without Matthew present to understand the options and process of transition. I would like to have been briefed on what involvement was expected from Matthew so I could have helped him prepare for the planning meetings.*

> *We needed an explanation at the outset of what the transition process entailed. The school did send us a pamphlet about the transition review but it wasn't very informative.*

Other ideas to improve transition planning meetings themselves included a legal obligation for key professionals to attend, and the use of an independent note-taker to record discussions and decisions.

The second set of suggestions concerned ways to improve the coordination of the process. A number of parents suggested that a named coordinator for each family would have been helpful, a role that will hopefully be taken on by Personal Advisers from the new Connexions Service as it is rolled out. Comments included:

> *Get one professional to own the planning process.*

> *Have a key person.*

> *It would have been more helpful to me as a parent if a coordinator could have been allotted to help with transition planning.*

> *To have a key person whose role is to advise parents on options – someone who will guide parents through the minefield of obstacles put in the way when trying to seek positive help.*

A third set of suggestions concerned the provision of information. Here, parents mentioned that it would be helpful to have experts to advise them, speakers from different agencies to talk to, resource packs for the young people and their parents to dip into when needed, examples of choices made by other students and links with other parents who had already been through the process.

> *Parents ought to know about everything. There ought to be an information pack really and then you can look at it when you're ready – when you reach that stage.*

> *All available options for a child leaving school should be presented, together with advantages and disadvantages.*

> *Provision of the catalogues listing various specialist college programmes would be very helpful in pointing parents in the right direction for locating the most appropriate provision.*

> *. . . database of available colleges.*

> *. . . maybe speak to someone who had gone through it the year before or so.*

> *Link with parents who have already been through the process.*

Other suggestions from parents for improving the transition process included: the provision of a half-way house for young people to ease their transition from school to more independent living; better attention paid to the transition from college; more flexible non age-related transfers to adult health and social services; and a better recognition of the individual needs of families at transition. For some families, especially those with a young person with a life-limiting impairment or medical condition, transition was a particularly difficult time that needed to be handled sensitively, yet this did not always happen.

Final comments from the young people

In part of our discussions with the young people in the study, we asked open ended questions about their experiences of growing up, what advice they might like to give to other young people growing up and what advice they might like to give to parents or professionals. A number of the young people mentioned things that could have improved the transition planning process for them, things that they had appreciated or messages that they would like to give to others.

On the whole, the young people had valued having consistent support and someone to talk things over with and to listen to them. One young person said that transition had been made easier by having people talk to her as well as people that she could talk to herself. Kath said that the advice that she would give someone else would be to:

. . . talk to other people when you feel lonely.

Kath was not alone in mentioning loneliness as an issue that made transition difficult. Several other young people indicated that growing up had been a lonely affair; one said that the best help that anyone could give would be in supporting him to keep in contact with all his friends, either through visits, phone calls, letters or emails.

The value of encouragement was also something that a number of the young people mentioned. Some wished they had been encouraged to do more things for themselves, that more had been expected of them or that they had been given harder work to do. One young man said that he had appreciated it when adults had started to trust him more and he had been given particular responsibilities. On the other hand, one young person had found the expectations overwhelming and asked that adults:

Help us a little bit more . . .

This highlights well the importance of treating each young person *as an individual*; this was a message that some of the young people felt particularly strongly about. One young man suggested that the most positive thing to do to help young people at transition was to 'take it slowly' at an individual pace; another valued the advocacy group that he belonged to that had supported him in making decisions and choices for himself; others mentioned the importance of having their own possessions around them and a sense of privacy and space. Finally, two of the young people focused on issues to do with self-confidence and the importance of a positive self-image. It is with one of these particularly pertinent comments that this chapter will end. It was directed to other young people with learning difficulties. Robert advised young people to:

Have faith in yourself . . . and say, this is me now, yeah!

Chapter 6: Key issues and examples of innovative practice

This chapter draws together the key findings of this study and explores their implications in the light of current policies. It also provides illustrations of services that are developing creative and innovative approaches to tackling transition. In weaving together the threads of the previous chapters, we focus in particular on:

- the transition planning process (including individual and strategic planning and multi-agency working)
- young people's involvement in planning
- the lack of choice in post-school options (including housing and employment)
- difficulties in accessing information about possible options
- the importance of peer relationships
- the needs of parent carers.

Binding together the key elements of a good transition experience are the five Cs: communication, coordination, comprehensiveness, continuity and choice, which are explored at the end of the chapter.

The transition planning process

This research has found:

- Young people with learning difficulties are continuing to leave the school system without any recognisable form of planning, despite legislation and guidance to the contrary.
- Lack of planning leads to uncertainty and stress for families.
- There was confusion, on the part of some parents, as to what a transition plan actually was.
- Even where young people *did* receive transition planning, some only received *ad hoc* planning, although others had a more consistent approach with plans being amended and updated as time moved on.

It is evident that widespread improvements are needed to the transition planning process. Despite a clear legislative and regulatory framework, some young people with learning difficulties leave school having had no transition planning that their parents are aware of. For other young people and their parents, the planning process is often characterised by confusion, a lack of coordination and poor liaison between agencies.

Planning at an individual level

The Government White Paper *Valuing People: a new strategy for learning disability for the 21st century* (DoH, 2001) advocates the development of a person-centred approach to planning, with explicit recognition of the priority that needs to be given to young people moving from children's to adult services. (According to the White Paper they should have access to person-centred planning by 2003.) There is an emerging consensus (as yet there is not a huge amount of formal evidence) that creative 'person-centred' planning can help generate new opportunities around individuals (see Sanderson et al, 1997). It remains to be seen how easy it will be to implement person-centred planning on a much larger scale and yet maintain the creativity and innovation that have been key characteristics hitherto. Nevertheless, there seems to be a good case for using *ideas* drawn from person-centred planning to improve the transition process. Oldham has been one of the earliest authorities to try and implement person-centred planning (see Box 3).[11]

Valuing People (DoH, 2001) also recognises the particular problems that may be experienced by young disabled people in getting their health care needs met as they move into adulthood. They are seen as a priority for the new system of Health Action Planning proposed by the White Paper, which for young people should be delivered through the transition planning process (see DoH, 2002a for more details).

Planning at a strategic level

As well as improving transition planning at an individual level, there is also a need to refine transition planning at a strategic level. To a large extent, *Valuing People* (DoH, 2001) recognises the need for better strategic planning and commissioning and much of the action specified by the White Paper is concerned with prompting this. For example, amongst other things, the newly formed Partnership Boards, which must have a transition champion, are meant to be:

- updating their Joint Investment Plans for learning disability services

- agreeing joint frameworks for person-centred planning, health action planning and quality assurance

---

11. Contact details for all the projects mentioned as examples of innovative or interesting work at transition are given in Appendix 3.

Box 3: Person-centred planning in Oldham

The aim of person-centred planning is to help individuals work out their aspirations, and then begin planning the process of achieving those aspirations. It is about planning 'life' (not just services), and is as much concerned with what might be possible as it is with what is available now. Perhaps most importantly, it tries to put the concerns of the individual and his or her family at the centre of the process, trying to organise it in ways that give them as much control as possible. That is the theory. Despite the stress placed on person-centred planning in the White Paper, as yet most local authorities have little or no experience of trying to implement it.

Oldham has more experience than most, and the experience gained in Oldham has played a significant part in shaping official guidance on person-centred planning (DoH, 2002b).

Oldham's strategy for doing person-centred planning has involved what they describe as 'breadth and depth'. Each year a significant number of staff from all services go on basic 'essential lifestyle planning'[12] courses. In addition, limited numbers of individuals have been sent on more advanced courses, designed to equip them with the skills and experience to actively facilitate person-centred planning in the locality. There is also an 'action learning' set for facilitators (a regular forum for people to continue learning from each other and to provide mutual support to improve practice).

Training is not limited to social services staff. People from the independent sector have also participated. Even more significantly, so have people with learning difficulties and families. In particular, a document called *Listen to me!*[13] has been used to support some self advocates to do their own planning. The hope is that some will eventually become trainers. Some family members have already joined the training team for the basic essential lifestyle planning course.

- developing strategies for housing and employment
- setting up a day service 'modernisation' programme.

This is a formidable agenda. While young people coming through the transition process are likely to benefit from these broader changes, arguably what is also needed is some kind of coherent strategy for transition, which

---

12. Essential lifestyle planning is just one of a number of 'styles' of person-centred planning. It is a way of organising things that tends to suit a wide range of people, and is relatively pragmatic in its focus.

13. *Listen to me!*, along with a range of other useful documents can be downloaded for free from the web site of the North West Development and Training Team. The address is: http://www.nwtdt.com There is a whole section of the site devoted to person-centred planning, with a subsection entitled families planning together.

would extend well beyond the existing transition planning framework. This would need to:

- tackle the issue of resources
- address issues in adult services in general, and in particular open up employment and supported living
- deal with specific areas of weakness (for example, the lack of suitable services for people from minority ethnic communities).

There are signs that some such strategies are beginning to emerge. For example, while neither authority would claim to have 'cracked it', both Surrey and Oldham have (in quite different ways) begun to put together a range of options that represent more than simply the sum of their parts (see Boxes 4 and 5).

Box 4: Strategic planning for transition in Surrey

The reason that Surrey began reviewing transition arrangements will be familiar to many authorities. Each year a new tranche of young disabled people were leaving school, yet many were not known to adult services until late in the day. There was often little opportunity to assess people properly (particularly people out of area in residential schools) and so there were few options other than maintaining existing placements. Transition was becoming a source of increasing pressure on the budget. Further, two conferences involving carers had revealed many criticisms (decisions made too late, no long-term planning, and people feeling they were 'left in the lurch'). All this prompted Surrey to take a much more strategic approach.

As a result Surrey:

- carried out a 'Best Value'[14] review of transition

The review used a range of methods to gather data, including a confidential questionnaire for families, focus groups with young people, a questionnaire for voluntary organisations (both locally and further afield), and interviews with a range of key stakeholders. At the same time, work on the local register of disabled children had identified that, each year for the foreseeable future, there were likely to be around 100 young people moving through the system, who would go on to be significant users of adult services, and for whom transition was likely to require intensive planning. Work with staff who knew these

---

14. 'Best Value' is a core part of Central Government's proposals for modernising local government. It requires each local authority to have a rolling programme for reviewing services within a framework that encourages the consideration not just of cost, but also quality and effectiveness. Significantly, in the case of Surrey, transition was an early focus for a Best Value review.

individuals, combined with some outline costs for different options, suggested that something approaching £2m would be needed each year to meet the needs of this group. One of the recommendations of the review was that these resources be added to the social services base budget and used within a commissioning strategy that would promote opportunities for independence.

• established a transition strategy steering group

This was a multi-agency group that also included the full range of critical social services players (commissioning, adult services, children's services, local care managers). Representatives from careers, education and health were there from the start, and there have been subsequent efforts to include representatives from housing (which the development of the local *Supporting People*[15] strategy has encouraged) with the aim of developing independent living options.

• worked with young people and families

Carers representatives are included on the transition strategy group. They were also directly involved in the Performance Review. One of the recommendations of the latter was that young people and families should be provided with much more information. At the same time, education and social services had jointly funded a two-year transition adviser post based with Mencap. This resulted in a booklet being sent to all families with a disabled child over 12, along with workshops for families, a video, and a website for young people. Similarly, the local Parents in Partnership group produced a short booklet that gave examples of 'thumbnail sketches' of people who had moved through transition, showing the kinds of options that might be possible. In addition, the Surrey User Network worked on 'communications passports'.

• began a process of 'modernising' adult services

As the transition process is being 're-jigged', adult services are themselves undergoing considerable change, with attempts to move away from the more limited combination of residential care and day services, towards more flexible alternatives. Even before *Valuing People* (DoH, 2001) had been published, the authority had decided to invest an extra £0.5m into a programme of change. Part of the wider strategy has been to try and ensure that young people are 'diverted' into opportunities for more independent living as early as possible. As a result three additional posts have been created, each providing a dedicated service for young people:

---

15. Supporting People is the proposed new framework for funding supported housing (replacing Transitional Housing Benefit) coming into place in 2003.

- a 'promoting independence' officer
- a mobility officer
- an employment officer.

In each case the post is designed to help care managers develop more appropriate packages of care. The authority has also been working with local colleges on a 'widening participation' project (which brought in additional resources), and a foyer style project (i.e. combining accommodation and training) is planned.

- developed an 'early identification' protocol

This aims to identify at 14+ the people who are likely to be significant users of adult services. At 16, this judgment is re-assessed, and if appropriate, an adult care manager will become involved. As yet, this is not happening consistently, but it does help to set up the final phase, where, each autumn there is a multi-agency meeting attended by an adult care manager.
A numbers of factors are considered to have helped move the whole process forward. These included:

- involving elected members in the process (including the Best Value review); as a result they were 'champions' of the strategy with the Council
- being able to use some solid data; this was critical in the argument for additional resources
- being able to develop a strategy that was perceived to be coherent
- pressure from families, who were an important driving force.

Box 5: Strategic planning for transition in Oldham

Oldham has developed a strategic approach to improving transition services with a range of initiatives. These include:

- An 'early referral' protocol

Referrals are accepted by the adult learning disability team at age 15 or 16 (rather than 18) for some specific groups, including young people with autistic spectrum disorders; with 'challenging behaviour'; with complex health care needs; and those who might require accommodation at age 18 or soon after.

The development of the protocol has not solved all problems (they still have the occasional crisis placement). However, it has made a positive impact, and it provides a focus for some of the other initiatives.

- Person-centred planning

According to *Valuing People* (DoH, 2001) services should increasingly be using person-centred planning approaches. Oldham has been one of the earliest authorities to try and implement person-centred planning, both in general, and as part of transition (see Box 3).

- The complex health care team

The complex health care team covers all ages, but one of the posts has a specific responsibility for working with young people in transition (particularly those identified through the early referral protocol).

The aim of the team is to provide support to people in everyday life and they try, as far as possible, to help individuals to access and use generic facilities and services (this prefigures the 'health facilitation' role highlighted in the White Paper). The complex health care team is a source of specialist knowledge for generic staff. For example, if an individual known to the team is admitted to hospital as an in-patient, ward staff can call on the team for advice. Increasingly, local generic health services are sending students on placement with the complex health care team.

It is recognised that there are negatives with having a specialist team, not least that there is a risk other services will see people with complex health needs as 'somebody else's responsibility'. However, in this case, it seems that the advantages more than outweigh any problems.

- Transition coordinator in supported employment

The local supported employment agency (TIE) has a post specifically dedicated to working with people in transition, funded using the Government's 'Promoting Independence' Grant. The post has been used to get work firmly on the agenda in special schools by developing and supporting work placements. The next challenge will be whether TIE can provide long-term support to some of the young people who have been able to access work experience for the first time.

- Ethnic minority action plan

Oldham has a large South Asian population, and there has long been recognition and awareness that minority ethnic communities were not being well served, with uptake of many services low. It seems that there were two aspects to this: the provision was not attractive to these communities, with services finding it difficult to engage with families, while families, for their part, often found the assessment process intrusive and unhelpful. Part of the problem involved having to rely on outside interpreters who did not share the value base of the services; part was due to the fears of families about the capacity of services to provide gender specific personal care services.

These concerns led to the development of the ethnic minority action plan, designed to try systematically to address the barriers faced by individuals and families from the South Asian community. This, in turn, resulted in the establishment of the Apqar Haq project, which was targeted at three distinct groups:

- current users (with the intention of improving the response)
- young people coming through transition
- people who were not using services or who had dropped out of services.

Apqar Haq was designed with a number of quite specific features. For example:
- it was locally based – the aim was to ensure the project had a physical presence in the communities being served, and efforts were put into building links with the local schools.
- bi-lingual link workers were recruited. Here the concern was to ensure that there was the chance to communicate directly with families, without the need to rely on an uncertain interpreting service. Link workers then worked with care managers to ensure that the needs of the families were understood. Subsequently a half-time bi-lingual administration worker was appointed.
- every effort was made to listen to, and learn from, families – traditional assessment formats were replaced by spending time with families and listening to their concerns. Person-centred planning techniques were used to try to ensure the individual and their families were at the centre of the process. Families were also consulted about staff training programmes established by the project. In addition the booklet *After age 16 – what next?* (Family Fund Trust, 1996) was translated into appropriate languages and distributed to local families.
- small scale pilot projects were established specifically to build trust.

To begin with, a 'supporting carers service' was set up, offering four hours of assistance at a time. Take-up for this service was good, so it was followed by larger scale short-break services which, amongst other things, provided gender specific weekends. These provided some early positive experiences of adult services for the young people and their families.

Lack of coordination between agencies

A fundamental problem with the transition planning process highlighted by the research is the lack of coordination and poor liaison between agencies. The revised Special Educational Needs Code of Practice (DfES, 2001a) (see Box 6) may go *some* way towards clarifying the transition planning process and ensuring a collaborative approach between agencies. However, it still leaves a degree of uncertainty about the structure of a transition plan and the transition planning process, particularly after Year 9.

Box 6: *The revised Special Educational Needs Code of Practice*

The revised Special Educational Needs Code of Practice (DfES, 2001a) states that:

The annual review in Year 9 and any subsequent annual reviews until the young person leaves school must include the drawing up and subsequent review of a Transition Plan. (9:51)

A representative of the Connexions Service, in most cases this is likely to be a PA, [Personal Adviser] must be invited to the Year 9 annual review meeting and, as a condition of the grant, must attend. (9:56)

However, no guidance is given as to the structure of a transition plan. Further, Personal Advisers (PAs) who will be responsible for coordinating its delivery, are not obliged to attend all subsequent annual reviews; they are 'expected to attend where appropriate' (9:56), 'should attend the review meeting in Year 11' (9:62) and should make 'every effort' to link the young person's assessment of their needs on leaving school with their transition plan (9:62). Nor are representatives of health and social services required to attend the Year 9 or subsequent planning meetings. The head teacher *must* invite a representative from social services to the Year 9 annual review meeting, and they 'should ensure that a social worker attends' (9:59). Health professionals involved in the management and care of the young person should, 'provide advice towards transition plans in writing and, wherever possible, attend the annual review meeting in Year 9' (9:60).

In recent years, a number of regional or area groups have been working together to develop joint transition policies in an attempt to unify their approach to transition planning. These have enhanced the transition planning process by:

- using an integrated assessment process

- developing a framework of good practice to enable transition planning meetings to focus on the whole needs of the young person within his/her family context

- fostering a coordinated approach to service provision

- encouraging assessments to incorporate long-term planning as opposed to re-active short-term responses.

One such project is the Eastern Region (SEN) Partnership Project, which is guided by a multi-disciplinary steering group (see Box 7). Another is the transition policy being developed in Plymouth by a multi-disciplinary group,

Box 7: The Eastern Region (Special Educational Needs) Partnership Project

Funded by the DfES, the Eastern Region (SEN) Partnership involves the 10 local authorities in the region working in partnership to support the education of pupils with SEN. Managed by a multi-agency steering group, the Partnership has, since its inception in April 1999, determined to take a strategic approach to addressing SEN issues.

The Partnership has taken forward a range of areas such as inclusion, demography/data collection, training and transition. It determined to focus on the latter because of concerns that transition planning was not being carried out systematically across the region.

Outcomes and outputs include:

- a regional transition plan which is now being piloted by four of the LEAs;
- 'Leaving School' – a regional directory of transition services for young people with SEN, which helps families understand the transition planning process and prepare themselves for meetings;
- protocols for the transition planning process for young people with statements of SEN;
- 'Planning for Connexions – transition for young people with SEN and/or disabilities – illustrative practice from the Eastern Region';
- a one-day conference: 'The Connexions service – transition from school to post-school provision for young people with learning difficulties and/or disabilities';
- a greater percentage of transition plans now being completed across the region.

For further information see the website: *www.hertsdirect.org/senregionalproject*

including head teachers, SEN coordinators, representatives from health and social services, Connexions and parents of people with learning difficulties. The resulting Transition Assessment, Transitional Annual Review and Personal Action Plan documents are currently being piloted by the local Connexions service. Overall, the intention is to provide a system that coordinates all professionals in the different elements (assessment, planning and implementation) of the transition process.

Young people's involvement in planning

This research has found:

- A substantial proportion of young people have little, if any, involvement in planning for their own future; almost a quarter (23%) were reported not to have been involved *at all*.

A striking inadequacy in the transition planning process for many of the young people in this research was a lack of meaningful participation in planning their own future. Facilitating student involvement seemed to be a key difficulty. The revised SEN Code of Practice states that:

The views of young people themselves should be sought and recorded wherever possible in any assessment, reassessment or review from Year 9 onwards. PAs, student counsellors, advocates or advisers, teachers and other school staff, social workers or peer support may be needed to support the young person in the transition process. (DfES, 2001a: 9:55)

Both the Code of Practice and the accompanying SEN Toolkit (DfES, 2001b) consider ways in which young people could be helped to participate fully in this process. This includes: curriculum planning focusing on activities that encourage pupils to reflect upon their own experiences and wishes and to form their own views; supporting young people with information, careers guidance, counselling, work experience and the opportunity to consider a range of options; making use of symbols, illustrative materials or Braille to communicate information; and drawing on the experience of any local pupil support or advocacy services for children which might be able to offer additional advice or assistance.

One innovative project that has recently started to address the issue of supporting young people to become fully involved in the transition process is the Trans-active Project led by Mencap. This is exploring the use of peer support to empower young people with learning difficulties in Birmingham and Lichfield to make independent choices about their future and to raise their expectations. The buddying scheme pairs young people with learning difficulties from special schools with their mainstream peers. Together, the young people spend time working on different topics relating to transition into adulthood, including advocacy, living skills, education, working, leisure and friendships. Multimedia are used to record their contributions.

The creative use of a variety of different media forms to help the young person to present their wishes is one way of promoting the fuller participation of young people with learning difficulties in the transition planning process. In the London boroughs of Westminster and Kensington & Chelsea, and in East London, Multimedia Profiling is being used, supported by the Acting Up organisation (see Box 8).

Box 8: Multimedia Profiling with Acting Up

Acting Up is a charity that works with people marginalised by severe communication difficulties to enable them to participate better in planning their own lives. It has developed Multimedia Profiling as a practical means to do this.

The Multimedia Profile is a computer-based catalogue of images, video film, sound recordings and text about a person's daily activities, personal history or preferences. Over a period of time, the profile builds into a user-centred resource that can be applied for a range of purposes. For example, in the boroughs of Westminster and Kensington & Chelsea, Multimedia Profiling is being introduced to support young people with learning difficulties make their views known at transition planning meetings. In Bromley Hall School in East London, Multimedia Profiling provides a means for young people who are moving from a special needs school to a local mainstream school to educate new staff and communicate their needs. The staff consider the profiles to be an excellent handover tool and a way to objectively measure progress from a baseline.

Evaluation of Multimedia Profiling suggests that it can help (paid) carers develop an understanding of young people's interests and communication skills and can be central to the person-centred planning process.

For further information see the website: www.acting-up.org.uk

Another way of promoting fuller participation by young people with learning difficulties is through the use of Communication Passports. The Surrey Users Network has a communication project in which project workers help young people to make their own 'communication passports' in filofax-type booklets. These give important information about the young person, such as their preferences, routines, interests and relationships, using symbols and/or photos. They have been used to help young people communicate with others, to provide information about them to others, and to support them in making choices for themselves. Pages are added in and taken out as necessary according to the young person's wishes and the changes in their life.

The lack of choice in post-school options

This research has found:

- The choice and range of provision was very limited for everyone.

- There is an assumption that people with learning difficulties will either remain in the family home or require residential care, with little creativity of thought about what other housing options might be suitable.

One of the most striking findings from this project was how little difference transition planning seemed to make to the young people's lives, particularly in relation to employment and housing opportunities. This was largely because there were so few options available. The lack of any real choice or options was a reason given by parents for why it was difficult for their children to participate in decision-making about their future; it was also, for many parents, the most negative thing about the planning process.

Some people are now questioning whether a focus on the transition planning process is the best way forward. Cumella and his colleagues (2000), for example, question whether *individual planning* itself can deliver the kinds of services that are needed; for them, the *lack of opportunities* for people with learning difficulties is the crucial issue. Key planks in any strategy to increase the opportunities available to young adults with learning difficulties must centre on employment and housing opportunities.

Employment opportunities

For many there is a danger that a period at college simply delays entry to more traditional forms of day services, or to unemployment. (Routledge 2000, p.21)

If an important aim is to help young people move on to employment, then the link between colleges and the employment services is critical. This could involve feedback mechanisms between schools, colleges and employment providers as to the interest and need for particular courses; involving employers in the design and content of college-based work preparation courses; and widening the scope of the college curriculum. One of the more long-standing examples of provision specifically designed to bridge the divide between college and employment is the Work Preparation Programme offered by the Bournemouth and Poole College (see Box 9).

Box 9: *Bridging the divide between colleges and the employment service in Bournemouth*

Bournemouth and Poole College provides a complex range of vocational and pre-vocational courses funded through the Learning and Skills Council. However, the Work Preparation Course is rather different from the rest of the provision: it is funded as a contract with the local Employment Services.

There are four modules within the programme:

- one-to-one guidance and advice
- personal development course
- job search skills course
- work experience placement and job coaches.

Time on the programme is limited but might typically involve a combination of four weeks personal development and three weeks job search skills, followed by a six-week (or two three-week) work placement.

This is a pan-impairment programme, so not all of those using the programme have a learning difficulty. Access to the course is through an assessment by a local Disability Employment Adviser.

The programme is demonstrably successful: between 60%–100% of the people completing the course move into paid employment.

Like Bournemouth and Poole College, Status Supported Employment Service has seen the link between college and work as important. However, they have also worked on the principle that the process of making links between young people and work needs to start even earlier, while the former are still at school. As a result, Status has been working on several pilot projects (see Box 10). These include: an 'Access to working life' programme, links to special schools and peer buddying and mentoring schemes.

Box 10: Status Employment pilot projects

- The Croydon College *Access to a working life* programme

The local college has established a 10-week course (two days a week) that incorporates the 'Workright' course accredited by ASDAN (Award Scheme Development and Accreditation Network). There are, however, a number of more innovative elements to the 'Access to a Working Life' course, including:

- the use of the Status at work pack, a resource developed locally with a range of partners
- three 'job samples' (i.e. taster experiences) supported by Status Employment consultants
- an exit strategy, in which all the students completing the course move on to the full supported employment service.

Effectively, one of the key early stages of supported employment has been integrated within the course; employment consultants come into college and work with students in order to work out where their interests and aptitudes lie (this is termed 'vocational profiling'). The result is an individualised action plan for each student that can be followed-up by Status Employment.

- Links to special schools

Status Employment has begun to work with two local special schools, with the aim of opening up work experience to a wider range of young people. Components of the programme include classroom-based work with the Status at work pack, access to a Status Employment consultant, job sample sessions alongside people who have already used Status services, and other activities designed to help provide a bridge to work. While some students were already trying work experience as part of the national curriculum, without the additional resources provided by Status Employment, such opportunities were limited. As with the links to college, the aim is to develop a partnership between the schools and Status Employment.

- Peer support

A key theme in the discussions with Status Employment was the notion that the people who use the service are a resource; they have something to offer too! For example, the experiences of workers went into the development of the Status at work pack. More specifically, Status Employment has increasingly begun to explore ways to offer peer support, through a combination of buddying and mentoring schemes. In this context, 'buddying' is more focused on learning the job, while mentoring implies a rather longer-term relationship, including the opportunity to talk to someone from a similar background about any fears or concerns.

Young people from both the special schools and the college are matched with people who have found a job. Status Employment provides support to the mentors, as well as arranging and supporting the work placements.

Aside from the moral support offered, the young people have the chance to do work experience with employers who are positive about employing disabled people. In turn, the buddies and mentors get a lot out of the experience, including recognition from the employer.

There is now well-documented evidence (see, for example, Mank et al, 1999 and 2000) that developing 'natural supports' (for example, support from colleagues) within the workplace can have a very positive impact. The buddying and mentoring schemes developed by Status Employment represent a way of extending some of those benefits to people involved in work experience. Such schemes are not confined to supported employment, but are part of the wider repertoire of many large employers (for example, Trust House Forte has a buddy system). For Status Employment, the process has been about thinking laterally and adapting existing practice, rather than doing something completely untried and untested.

So far, these schemes run by Status Employment are in the development phase. However, the pilots have been so successful that the organisation is looking for some longer-term funding to consolidate the ideas. Although it is usually possible to get short-term funding for such innovative ideas, it is often hard to find ways of funding their longer-term implementation. Accessing suitable funding is likely to be critical in enabling significant local development of opportunities. In the case of employment related services this will probably need to include:

- being an approved provider for both local social services departments and employment services

- having the capacity to draw on a diverse range of funding sources

- keeping costs low.

Developing partnerships across the education/work boundary is probably going to be one of the ways that providers will be able to access the full range of funding opportunities. However, many of the funding streams are complex, far from transparent, and 'partial' in that they only cover some aspects of the support that young people might need. The demands of different funding streams inevitably impose limitations on all providers, and a mutual understanding of those limitations is important. In particular, there are risks of 'perverse incentives' arising; for example, the young person who gets offered a job on the basis of a job 'sample' or taster (and who therefore does not complete a course) may well represent lost funding to a college. Additionally, there may be a danger of:

- focusing on people who are likely to be easy to place

- the negotiation of unambitious objectives

- hesitancy in the recruitment of new staff if there is not a long-term guaranteed flow of funding (the evidence is that it takes time to develop the skills and links to be really effective)

- being hampered by the rigidities between provision contracted through the Disability Service Teams (for example, Workstep) and the New Deal provision (moving from one to another does not count as a successful 'outcome' for funding purposes, even though this might be a helpful step for the individual).

If more young people with learning difficulties are to have better access to a range of employment opportunities, there will have to be a clear strategic link between social care and employment services. By implication this has been recognised by the Government in its requirement for local authorities to develop Joint Investment Plans for Welfare to Work services. However, we sometimes found a degree of scepticism on the ground as to how much difference this initiative will really make. Aside from their complexity, there were concerns that these Joint Investment Plans are still very dominated by a social care, rather than an employment, perspective.

One example of an interesting link between the voluntary sector, social care, education and employment services is in Harrogate, where Barnardo's run a successful training restaurant and coffee shop for young people with a range of learning needs, most of whom then move on to permanent employment. The scheme has close links with a number of agencies: the Learning and Skills Council pay a training allowance to the young people plus support costs, and social services provide placement fees for mature trainees who require a more lengthy stay at Dr B's. The scheme is linked to a supported lodgings project nearby, which provides the students with supported accommodation should they need it (see Box 11).

Box 11: Barnardo's Supported Lodgings for Young People in Harrogate

Barnardo's Grove Road Project organises the Supported Lodgings for Young People (SLYP) Scheme in Harrogate. The scheme offers young people aged 16–24 a choice of lodgings, and acts as a stepping-stone between home, foster care or college and more independent living.

Young people are offered accommodation in ordinary homes with approved lodgings providers. Scheme workers recruit, train and support lodgings providers, and make suitable links between the lodgings providers and young people. They also provide support to the young people using the scheme, to enable them to develop their potential and maximise their independence.

Housing opportunities

As with much else, the housing opportunities available to young people are likely to be shaped by the inadequacies of adult services. As Hatton (2001) states:

- there is under-provision of housing and support in relation to demand

- there are huge geographical variations in the quantity and the nature of housing and support services

- there are inequalities in access to, and provision of, housing related support across different ethnic groups

- there is little opportunity for moving out of the family home for people with learning difficulties; opportunities are dictated more *by the age of the family carer* than by the age of the disabled person, unless there is some form of crisis.

Despite a widespread interest in ideas about 'independent' living (often referred to as supported living – see Simons and Ward, 1997), most services still take the shape of some form of residential care or group home (see Harker and King, 1999; DoH, 1999). In this context, it was perhaps unsurprising to find so few examples of innovative housing and support initiatives targeted specifically at young people moving through transition (see Box 11 above for a positive exception).

One of the objectives of *Valuing People* (DoH, 2001) is to widen the range of options open to people with learning difficulties. However, in the case of housing, there is a danger that the aspirations of some young people will be thwarted, as the priorities set out in the White Paper are focused on people living with elderly family carers. Young people who are not at immediate risk, and who do not live with elderly family carers, will inevitably continue to be a relatively low priority. While this may be the reality, it is certainly not a desirable situation. Low priority should not, after all, equal no priority. It is important that local commissioners explore ways of opening up new housing opportunities. Further, when Partnership Boards develop their housing strategy, the needs of young people should be specifically addressed.

Developing a much wider range of housing and support opportunities generally, is likely to be a significant challenge for commissioners. As part of a new Department of Health funded project on strategic change, the Norah Fry Research Centre has established a website specifically for commissioners.[16] It is no accident that the first content to be posted on the site has focused on developing housing and support strategies (see Simons, 2001). Such a strategy is likely to involve two critical strands:

1) Ensuring that young people and their families have the maximum possible information about what is *possible*

Aside from the *Plain facts*[17] accessible research findings series that includes several issues on housing options, other accessible material about housing and support options targeted specifically at people with learning difficulties include:

- the video pack *Make your move* (Holman, 1998)

- *Making housing choices* (King and Harker, 2000a), which includes an accessible section

- *Get moving! Making a choice about where to live* (Foundation for People with Learning Disabilities, 2001) – a booklet specifically written for people living at home with their families

- *Your place to live* (Wood and Hall, 2001), which includes a video and accessible written material, along with resources for care managers.

Families are likely to find useful the range of information developed by the *Housing Options* advisory service, which can be downloaded free from their website.[18] Other material specifically designed for carers includes the video and publication *Room to move* (Cowen, 2001) and *Leaving home, moving on* (King and Harker, 2000b). Of particular value may be material which helps explore options that involve less reliance on services, such as the booklet by King (2001) on using parental equity.[19]

---

16. http://www.bris.ac.uk/Depts/NorahFry/Strategy/
17. http://www.bris.ac.uk/Depts/NorahFry/PlainFacts/index.html
18. http://www.hoptions.demon.co.uk/
19. Parental equity involves using the value of one's own property to make housing provision for one's son or daughter with learning difficulties

2) Making creative, sustainable use of the new funding opportunities offered by Transitional Housing Benefit (THB) and subsequently (after 2003) the *Supporting People* framework

Although it will be possible to combine *Supporting People* money in more intensive support packages alongside community care budgets, it is primarily targeted at people who need less intensive support. It *could* be used creatively for young people at transition who are currently marginalised by social services eligibility criteria. However, the issues are complex. For those unfamiliar with convolutions of these new funding systems, the paper by Miller (2001) may be of use.

The difficulties in accessing information about possible options

This research found:

- At all stages of the transition process, parents were struggling to get accurate information about a wide range of issues or options – from information on specific things such as benefits or housing options, to knowing who to approach with their questions, and how to get hold of them.

- Information appropriate for the young people was even scarcer that that for their parents.

- Few, if any, young people made fully informed decisions about their future direction in life.

A number of organisations and authorities have developed, or are in the process of producing, transition packs or information files for young people and their parents as they approach school-leaving age. These share a common aim of helping families through transition by giving clear information about the services and issues that will affect them at this time. The East Surrey Transition Project, for example, has produced a booklet called *Options for the Future* (2000) for young disabled people locally. At a national level, the Family Fund Trust has produced *After 16 – what's new?* (Family Fund Trust, 1999), a general guide to the opportunities that are available to young disabled people as they reach age 16, with information on a range of issues such as education, benefits, sources of advice and practical help. A companion booklet called *Your Life, Your Future* (Boddy, 2001) provides information specifically for young people.[20] Action 19+, an alliance of national and regional voluntary bodies, has also produced some helpful information, including an information pack for disabled people, their

---

20. This publication is also available on the internet at: http: www.after16.org.uk

advocates and carers called *19+: a guide to getting what you need from your local authority at 19+* (Action 19+, 2001).

Although such sources of information are welcome, there is also a clear need for an information strategy within each local authority; a system by which personnel can keep up to date with a whole range of options, across all the different sectors, and through which information can be disseminated. Coupled with this, must be the facility to deliver information in a variety of ways; from written material, to workshops and seminars, drama productions and computer programs. The involvement of young people and families in the development of such information is crucial, so that it is appropriate, accessible and functional.

The importance of peer relationships

This research found:

- One of the most critical things that made transition difficult for the young people was loneliness. Several young people indicated that growing up had been a lonely affair; one said that the best help that anyone could give would be in supporting him to keep in contact with all his friends.

- Families recognised the importance of friendships, but parents and young people alike needed information, advice and support with many issues around developing and maintaining friendships.

- No matter how accepting or otherwise parents were about their son or daughter developing sexual relationships, many of them felt at a loss as to where to go for advice or support in talking through the issues.

- Peer relationships were important for giving young people higher expectations, self-esteem and encouragement.

- There was a need to build on young people's already established networks of friends.

- There was a need for appropriate role models, mentors and support groups for young people with learning difficulties at transition.

The issue of friendships was one that was prominent in most of the young people's interviews. It was also apparent that the whole issue of friendships and relationships was problematic for many parents. Social support, particularly peer relationships, together with the development of social skills are important in helping young people move towards adulthood, yet many of the young people experienced difficulties in maintaining contact with friends when they moved on to new service provision, and in negotiating roles and boundaries within relationships.

One strategy might be to work with young people in mapping their friendships and planning ways to maintain and sustain key relationships over the transition period. Access to information would also help. One innovative service set up to provide information and support around sexuality to young people with learning difficulties and their families at transition is the Connect Project in Bradford (see Box 12).

Box 12: Barnardo's Connect Project in Bradford

Barnardo's Connect Project aims to help people with learning difficulties exercise their right to be sexual people and to be better protected from sexual abuse. Focusing particularly on young people with learning difficulties, it works in three, inter-dependent, ways:

- direct work with young people with learning difficulties themselves
- work with parents and carers to raise awareness of the right of their son or daughter to a sexual life and to be protected from sexual abuse - and to help them voice any concerns
- the planning and implementation of staff training programmes in this area.

The project workers are also key players in the local Sexuality and Learning Disability Forum, a monthly meeting of workers, carers and People First, who aim to develop better practice, policy making and service delivery in this multi-cultural area. In recent years, they (together with local parents) have organised two one-day conferences for professionals and parents on the theme 'It's only natural'; they have produced a video resource (with supporting booklet) with the local health authority; and have published a book, *Holding on: letting go – sex, sexuality and people with learning disabilities* (Drury, J., et al. 2000).

The needs of parent carers

This research found:

- Fewer than half of the parents who were aware of transitional planning while their son or daughter was as school reported that their own need for information (so that they could help their son or daughter consider their options) was recognised.

- A significant degree of unhappiness and stress was experienced by many parents in seeking appropriate options for their son or daughter.

- There is a need for more effective involvement of families in the transition planning process.

The Carers and Disabled Act 2000, which came into force in England in April 2001, gives parents and carers (who are supporting someone over the age of 18) an enhanced right to an assessment of their own needs. In addition, social services departments are now able to provide carers with direct payments of cash with which to make their own support arrangements, instead of receiving direct services provided through the local authority.[21] Such services are not defined in the Guidance to the Act, but should 'maintain the health and well-being of the carer'. Few of the parents in our study were aware of this; indeed, only a quarter noted that their own support needs were considered in any way.

Inevitably, there is a potential tension between the needs and rights of parent carers and other family members, and the needs and rights of their disabled children. What we found, however, was that most, if not all, of the parents in our study had given considerable time, thought and energy to the needs of their sons and daughters, whilst lacking support themselves. One example of a service that provides practical support for the parents and siblings of young people with learning difficulties in its residential provision is that of Sunfield, a residential school in the West Midlands. They have a Family Charter, a document distributed to all families stating what support the family should expect. This includes practical support such as providing a private space for the family to spend time together; access to a family library/resource centre; the opportunity for making links with other families and events for siblings. Emotional support is provided by making regular contact with parents, having care and concern for their parenthood and valuing the parents' opinions and knowledge of their child.

Not only were the parent carers in our study lacking support for themselves and other family members, most also felt that they did not actively participate as equals in the transition planning process. Parents did not always feel that professionals were open with information, valued their knowledge and experience, or communicated with them on an equal basis, treating them as active partners.

Involving parents more in the transition planning process could be achieved through the wider availability of parent workshops, informing parents about all aspects of transition. Such workshops are run in a number of areas by the Home Farm Trust (see Box 13). Courses such as these help empower parent

---

21. The Act also entitles young disabled people – aged 16 or 17 – themselves to receive direct payments instead of services. (For further information on accessing direct payments for people with learning difficulties, see Holman and Bewley, 1999; Bewley, 2002).

Box 13: The Home Farm Trust's transition workshops for parents and siblings

As a response to perceived need, the Home Farm Trust (HFT) Carer Support Service has developed, run, evaluated and sought local ownership of eight-week courses specifically for parents whose sons or daughters are moving into (or within) the transition phase.

Courses are developed on a local authority wide basis, in conjunction with personnel from statutory authorities, voluntary groups and young people who use local services (all of whom present material). The workshop-based courses:

- provide information to parents
- enable self-help support to share and explore the emotional challenges parents face
- increase parents' opportunities to hear the views of young disabled people who have experienced transition
- encourage participants to share the information with their own sons and daughters
- support the production of user-friendly local transition materials for young people and their parents
- provide a focus for local professionals with specific responsibilities for collaboratively managing services around this time – whilst also exposing them to the day-to-day issues experienced by young people and their families, so helping to inform the planning process.

The programme includes sessions on:

- an overview of transition
- education legislation and local transition planning procedures
- social service assessments and provision relating to children and adults
- further education and supported employment possibilities, and the role of careers advisers/Connexions
- benefits changes at age16 and sources of independent advice
- housing opportunities
- health provision – moving over to adult services
- leisure facilities and voluntary sector support.

carers and increase their knowledge-base and confidence, through the provision of information and the coming together of a supportive network.

Another example of parental involvement is provided by APASENTH (Asian Parents Association for Special Educational Needs in Tower Hamlets) which has developed from a modest informal parents group to a registered charity, providing a wide range of services to Asian and Bangladeshi young people and their family carers (see Box 14).

Box 14: APASENTH (Asian Parents Association for Special Educational Needs in Tower Hamlets)

Set up in 1984 by parents, APASENTH has pioneered a number of culturally appropriate services to support Bangladeshi children and young people plus their family carers. These include:

- day services (with linked college courses)
- home-care and short break services
- welfare rights provision
- an integrated training and disability employment support programme
- health awareness promotion
- volunteer and training placements
- regular family carer support groups.

In addition, a Special Educational Needs (SEN) Development Worker for Bangladeshi children in special schools is seconded to work at APASENTH three days a week during term time. As she is known to all Bangladeshi families with a family member in a special school, the families are able to approach transition with the support of someone familiar, who is of their culture, and who is aware of post-school issues and options. Home visits, pre-transition preparation, support at meetings and visits to possible provision are all part of the service offered. As the LEA facilitate further SEN inclusion, the Development Worker will help to ensure that young people and their families receive the support they need.

APASENTH is based in a community arts and social centre. It forms a focus for Bangladeshi families with a disabled relative and their services are often commissioned by the local authority, which uses them for consultative work.

The need for five Cs – communication, coordination, comprehensiveness, continuity and choice

This study has uncovered serious shortcomings in the transition arrangements for young people with learning difficulties and their families. It has highlighted a catalogue of inadequacies and the effects that these have had on families. We have tried to balance this with some positives: with what parents and their youngsters say would help most; what the elements of a good transition experience might be; and with examples of services that are developing creative and innovative approaches to transition in their area.

Binding together the key elements of a good transition experience are the five Cs: communication, coordination, comprehensiveness, continuity and choice.

Communication:
- open, honest, timely and respectful communication between agencies – and between agencies and families
- independent advocacy for young people.

Coordination:
- effective inter-agency working
- joint training initiatives
- joint assessment procedures
- a cohesive strategic approach to service provision.

Comprehensiveness:
- a system for ensuring that *all* young people with learning difficulties have an effective transition plan, as required by legislation and guidance
- appropriate race and disability equality training for all staff
- an expectation that young people with learning difficulties and their families will have access to the same opportunities to realise their aspirations as their (non disabled) peers.

Continuity:
- the availability of key workers to support individual youngsters and their families throughout the transition phase
- a seamless transition from children's to adult services (in health, social services, education, housing and the voluntary sector)
- the availability of a range of options for young people to move into and between.

Choice:
- more – and better – involvement of young people with learning difficulties (and their families) in the transition planning process
- access to appropriate information for young people and their families on potential options available

- the development of a range of local post-school alternatives in housing and employment (including measures to tackle the particular barriers to more independent living faced by young people with learning difficulties).

In this report we have presented the (often poor) experiences of young people with learning difficulties and their families at transition, their ideas on what would make things better, and some examples of good, or at least better, practice in a number of areas. It is only if services – and the staff within them – have the will and determination to make transition a better experience, and are prepared to take on board the ideas of young people with learning difficulties and their families (like those presented here), that youngsters and their families will be able to look to the future with some optimism – and not see adulthood as a dark cloud lurking.

Summary

The transition to adulthood can be a difficult time for all young people and their families, but young people with learning difficulties face additional challenges. A questionnaire survey of 283 families and in-depth interviews with 27 young people and 27 parent carers in England, undertaken by the Home Farm Trust and the Norah Fry Research Centre, found that despite legislation and guidance:

- A fifth of youngsters had left school *without* a transition plan
- Almost half the young people had little or no involvement in the planning for their future
- Lack of planning led to uncertainty and stress for some families
- The quality of transition planning varied widely; in some cases it was ad hoc, confused and uncoordinated
- The topics covered in transition planning were often quite different from those families considered to be important
- For many young people, key issues (eg. transfer to adult health or social services) had still not been addressed by the time they left school
- Whether or not youngsters had received transition planning made little difference to what happened to them after leaving school
- There were few post-school options available to young people particularly in relation to housing and employment
- There was a lack of easily accessible information for parents and young people about what future possibilities might be
- Concerns raised by the young people and their families which inhibited greater independence focused on:
    - personal safety and risk
    - money matters (including benefits)
    - transport.

Background

Moving into adulthood is one of the most far-reaching and complex transitions for anyone, but young people with learning difficulties face additional challenges including transfer from children's to adult health and social services.

The particular problems confronted by young people with learning difficulties and their families were recognised in the English White Paper *Valuing People* (DoH, 2001); objective 2 focuses specifically on transition to adult life. The new Partnership Boards, established to oversee local implementation of the White Paper are supposed to include a transition champion, while the new Connexions service should ensure that every young person will have a Personal Adviser to help them negotiate leaving school and entering adult life (DfEE, 2000).

The official duty to undertake transition planning was set out in the Education Act 1993 and associated Code of Practice (DfEE, 1994), revised and updated in 2001 (DfES, 2001a).

The research

The study sought to establish whether legislation and guidance were being followed for young people with learning difficulties and their families at transition.

- A postal questionnaire was sent to 370 families (283 replied: a 76% response rate), asking about their experiences of transition planning, the aspirations of the young people and their parent carers, the outcomes of the process and how far these reflected the views of young people and their families. The young people were aged 13–25, so were at different stages in the transition process.

- In consultation with groups of young people with learning difficulties, a *Growing Up* workbook was developed and used to interview 27 young people with learning difficulties.

- In-depth interviews were also carried out with 27 parents.

- Visits were made to 10 projects across England which seemed to be addressing key concerns and demonstrating elements of good practice at transition.

How many young people had transition plans?

Annual transition planning meetings should be held for all young people with learning difficulties in year 9 (over the age of 14). Although the majority of parents felt there was a need for school-led planning, the survey found that:

- Only two-thirds of those still at school had a transition plan

- A fifth had left school without a plan (despite the fact that the majority had left when planning was already a legal requirement)

- The proportion of youngsters leaving school *without* a plan had *increased* between 1998 and 2000.

Young people's involvement in planning for their future

He found the process very unsettling and he was bewildered because he did not appear to know what was going on.

Legislation and guidance direct that the young person's views must be sought and recorded during their transition planning, but the study found that:

- only 29% had been very much involved

- 29% had been partly involved

- 19% had little involvement

- 23% of young people were not involved *at all*.

Young people still at school were *less likely* to have been involved in their transition planning than those who had already left and were also *less likely* to have had their views reflected in their plans.

Young people were *more likely* to be able to make choices when work experience or link placements could help them make informed choices, when they could look at videos or brochures about possible options, and when planning timescales allowed them to emotionally adjust to future changes.

Issues covered in transition plans

Almost everything concerned with my daughter's education and different possibilities for life beyond school I have had to find out for myself through friends and searching through different organisations. At times it has proven to be a long and painful experience. At no time has information been readily available.

The transition plan should touch on every aspect of the young person's future life. But there was a significant discrepancy between issues that families wanted to be addressed (information on leisure and social opportunities, benefits, future housing options and further education opportunities were the topics most wanted) and those which were actually covered in transition planning (only further education, of the above four topics).

Does transition planning make a difference?

The move to adulthood involves a number of key transitions for young people with learning difficulties. Whether or not they had received transition planning seemed to make little difference to what happened to youngsters in the study.

College, employment or other day activities

Over three-quarters of the young people went directly from school into further education (over half of these to residential colleges), often because this seemed to be what was expected rather than something the young person might choose to do. Very few had worked on a paid or voluntary basis; about a quarter were using day (resource and activity) centres.

We didn't realise Kath could stay at college 'til 25, we only found out about that later on . . . it gives you a breathing space to find out if there is anything.

That was lovely when he got his first wage slip . . . it was the most wonderful moment, he was so proud.

Moving into their own home

Almost three-quarters of youngsters who had left school were still living in the family home. Although most parents wanted housing options to be included in the transition planning process, only one in ten who had had some planning felt that this had been covered well. Families need information and support to negotiate this major transition but where the young person had moved away from home, this was largely due to the often stressful efforts of parents themselves.

Living with my parents . . . I like that, it's good. I'd like to [move out one day] but I'd have to think about it and talk it over with my parents.

Adult social activities, friendships and relationships

Although leisure and social activities was the topic that the largest number of parents wanted covered in planning, this had *not* been covered for over half the families in their transition planning. Many of the young people's friendship networks were repeatedly disrupted after they left school. Parents themselves were often trying to organise structured activities for their sons or daughters, but were doing so with little information or support, particularly in the area of adult relationships.

> *I mean, you know, we thought we had problems when she was younger but this is getting out of our territory really. We really don't quite know how to handle it.*

The move from paediatric to adult health services

The revised Code of Practice sets out a clear role for health services' involvement in transition planning and *Valuing People* (DoH, 2001) identifies young people at transition as a priority group to receive individual Health Action Plans in the future.

Over half the parents who had received transition planning reported that transfer to adult health services had not been covered at all, and less than a fifth thought it had been covered well. For parents, adult health services meant a lack of continuity and of regular reviews.

> *While Sarah was under the care of child services it was consistent. It was a very good consultant ... when we were handed over to adults ... every time we went we seemed to see a different person. And we'd spend half the appointment going over past history. The continuity had gone completely.*

The move from children's to adult social services

For more than 40% of families who had received some transition planning, transfer to adult social services had not been dealt with at all; only a quarter felt it had been covered well. This lack of effective links between children's and adult's services was highlighted by *Valuing People*.

> *I think it was when she was 19 when she [the social worker for the children's team] said 'I won't be coming any more and I doubt very much if you will see much of the people who are taking over from me'.*

Factors inhibiting greater independence

Several issues were mentioned during the in-depth interviews, which affected the extent to which the young people could exercise greater independence in their lives.

Safety and risk

Concerns about safety and risk were spontaneously mentioned by half the parents. A quarter of the young people had experienced serious incidents including severe bullying and sexual assault (though action against the perpetrators had rarely been taken); others expressed concern about personal safety including road safety. Some parents acknowledged they might be 'over-protective' but their fears and anxiety were sadly sometimes justified.

> *I want to know there's people about . . . in case someone came to me and have a go at you.*

> *They've shown me how to cross the road and I've done it once or twice on my own but I still don't feel safe.*

Money and benefits

Irrespective of their age, few of the young people managed their own money or knew how to budget; parents often did this on their behalf, although some were aware that work on this could enhance their son or daughter's independence.

> *Ah money – I can sort it out all right. It's just when I go to buy things I don't get it right.*

Young people may be entitled to claim certain benefits when they reach the age of 16, but over half the parents who had received transition planning or whose children had left school said that benefits issues had not been covered at all. Nearly three-quarters of parents who had not been through the planning process saw this as an important issue.

> *[Claiming benefits] was like [being] in the middle of a maze . . . you're going round and round and back.*

Transport

Almost three-quarters of parents whose children were still at school wanted post-school transport arrangements to be covered in the transition plan, but many found their hopes were frustrated in that such discussions were discouraged until prospective service changes had been definitely agreed.

Parents had many concerns about letting young people travel independently and some of the young people voiced concerns about the unpredictability of public transport.

I'd like to learn to use the bus, yes.

Young people's views on improving the transition experience

The young people in the study suggested ways of improving the transition planning process, mentioned things they had appreciated, and had messages to pass on to others. These included:

- having someone independent who they could talk things over with and who would listen to them

- having consistent support to enhance their self-confidence and self-esteem

- being treated as an individual

- others encouraging them to having higher (but not overwhelming) expectations of themselves

- being given more responsibility and privacy.

Have faith in yourself . . . and say, this is me now, yeah!

. . . talk to other people when you feel lonely.

Parents' views on the transition planning process

Parents described positive and negative aspects of transition planning and suggested changes to the process which they would like to see.

Positive aspects included:
- Work experience or link placements to adult services and opportunities for the young person which provided new experiences, time to adjust to new places and helped them exercise choices

- The young person being able to make informed choices

- Allowing time for the young person to 'emotionally prepare' for change

- Staff in school or adult services who were supportive, encouraging and acted in the young person's best interests

- Being actively involved themselves in the planning process.

Suggestions for improvement included:

- Initiating transition planning reviews at the prescribed time
- Regular review meetings to revisit and update the plan
- Advice and guidance on preparing for meetings
- Ensuring that all key professionals attend review meetings
- A transparent transition process with clear accountability
- Provision of accurate, up-to-date information in a range of formats
- A named coordinator for each family.

Better practice at transition?

Bridging the Divide also found illustrations of creative and innovative initiatives in a variety of geographical locations across England, which were starting to address the problems described by parents and young people in the study. Between them they exemplified the five Cs:

The five Cs: elements in a good transition experience

Communication
which is open, honest and respectful between agencies, and between agencies and families; independent advocacy for young people.

Coordination
effective inter-agency working; joint training initiatives; joint assessment procedures and a cohesive strategic approach to service provision.

Comprehensiveness
an effective transition plan for *all* young people; appropriate race and disability equality training for all staff; expectation that young people with learning difficulties will have access to the same opportunities to realise their aspirations as their peers.

Continuity
key workers to support individual youngsters and their families throughout the transition process; a seamless transition from children's to adult services; a range of options for young people to move into and between.

Choice

more and better involvement of young people and their families in the transition process; access to appropriate information on potential options; development of a range of local post-school alternatives in housing and employment.

References

Action 19+ (2001) *19+ A guide to getting what you need from your Local Authority at 19 plus*, Action 19+: London.

Azmi, S., Emerson, E., Caine, A. & Hatton, C. (1996) *Improving services for Asian people with learning disabilities and their families*, The Mental Health Foundation: London.

Baxter, C., Poonia, K., Ward, L. & Nadirshaw, Z. (1990) *Double discrimination. Issues and services for people with learning difficulties and their families from black and ethnic minority groups*, Kings Fund/CRE: London.

Bewley, C. (2002) *Pointers to control (2nd edition)*, Values into Action: London.

Boddy, L. (2001) *Your life, your future*, The Family Fund Trust: York.

Chamba, R., Ahmad, W., Hirst, M., Lawton, D. & Beresford B. (1999) *On the edge: minority ethnic families caring for a severely disabled child*, The Policy Press: Bristol.

Cowen, A. (2001) *Room to move: a book for parents of young people with learning disabilities leaving home*, Joseph Rowntree Foundation: York.

Cumella S., Reybekil, N., de Mesurier, N. & Tischler, V. (2000) Transition to adulthood: a policy failure (abstract), *Journal of Intellectual Disability Research*, 44, 3&4, 251.

Department for Education and Employment (1994) *Code of practice on the identification and assessment of special educational needs*, HMSO: London.

Department for Education and Employment (2000) *Connexions: the best start in life for every young person*, DfEE: London.

Department for Education and Skills (2001a) *Special educational needs: code of practice*, DfES Publications: London.

Department for Education and Skills (2001b) *SEN toolkit,* DfES Publications: London.

Department of Health (1989) *The Children Act*, HMSO: London.

Department of Health (1992) *Social care for adults with learning disabilities (mental handicap)*. Circular (92) 15.

Department of Health (1999) *Facing the facts. Services for people with learning difficulties: a policy impact study of social care and health services*, Department of Health Publications: London.

Department of Health (2001) *Valuing people: A new strategy for learning disability in the 21st century*, Department of Health Publications: London.

Department of Health (2002a) *Action for health – health action plans and health facilitation*, Department of Health Publications: London.

Department of Health (2002b) *Planning with people: towards person centred approaches – guidance for implementation groups*, Department of Health Publications: London.

Drury, J., Hutchinson, L. & Wright, J. (2000) *Holding on: letting go – sex, sexuality and people with learning disabilities*, Souvenir Press: London.

East Surrey Transition Project (2000) *Options for the future: a what, when and how guide for parents as young disabled people make the transition to adult life*, East Surrey Transition Project.

Family Fund Trust (1999) *After age 16 – what's new? Choices and challenges for young disabled people*, The Family Fund Trust: York. (This is a revised and enlarged edition of the Family Fund Trust's former publication: *After age 16 – what next?*)

Flynn, M. & Hirst, M. (1992) *This year, next year, sometime. . .? Learning disability and adulthood*, National Development Team: Manchester.

Foundation for People with Learning Disabilities (2001) *Get moving! Making a choice about where to live*, Foundation for People with Learning Disabilities: London.

Harker, M. & King, N. (1999) *An ordinary home: housing and support for people with learning difficulties*, Local Government Association: London.

Hatton, C. (2001) *Strategies for change. Developing housing and support. Briefing papers: lessons from research*, Norah Fry Research Centre: Bristol. http://www.bristol.ac.uk/Depts/NorahFry/Strategies/

Hirst, M. & Baldwin, S. (1994) *Unequal opportunities: growing up disabled*, HMSO: London.

Holman, A. (1998) *Make your move: a video guide to independent living*, Values Into Action: London.

Holman, A. & Bewley, C. (1999) *Funding freedom 2000: people with learning difficulties using direct payments*, Values Into Action: London.

Khan, J., Cohen, R. & O'Sullivan, T. (1998) *Young Adults Transition Project*. Optimum Health Services NHS Trust. (Unpublished working paper. Tel: 0207 771 4510 for copies or information.)

King, N. (2001) *Using parental property to provide future housing for people with learning disabilities: guidance for families and advisors*, The Foundation for People with Learning Disabilities: London.

King, N. & Harker, M. (2000a) *Making housing choices: housing options for people with learning difficulties*, Pavilion Publishing: Brighton.

King, N. & Harker, M. (2000b) *Leaving home, moving on: housing options for people with learning disabilities in the UK*, Foundation for People with Learning Disabilities: London.

Mank, D., Cioffi, A., & Yovanoff, P. (1999) Impact of co-worker involvement with supported employees on wage and integration outcomes, *Mental Retardation*, 37, 5, 383–394.

Mank, D., Cioffi, A. & Yovanoff, P. (2000) Direct support in supported employment and its relation to job typicalness, co-worker involvement and employment outcomes, *Mental Retardation*, 38, 6, 506–516.

The Mental Health Foundation (1996) *Building expectations: opportunities and services for people with a learning disability*, The Mental Health Foundation: London.

Miller, N. (2001) *Strategies for change 'Developing housing and support' briefing papers: the implications of Supporting People*, Norah Fry Research Centre: University of Bristol. http://www.bristol.ac.uk/Depts/NorahFry/Strategies/

Mir, G., Nocon, A., Ahmad, W. & Jones, L. (2001) *Learning difficulties and ethnicity*, Department of Health: London.

Mitchell, W. (1999) Leaving special school: the next step and future aspirations, *Disability & Society* 14, 6, 753–770.

Morris, J. (1999) *Hurtling into a void*, Pavilion Publishing/Joseph Rowntree Foundation: Brighton.

Morrow, V. & Richards, M. (1996) *Transitions to adulthood: a family matter?* Joseph Rowntree Foundation: York.

Pearson, M., Flynn, M., Maughan, J. & Russell, P. (1999) *Positive health in transition*, National Development Team: Manchester.

Robinson, C. & Williams, V. (2000) *In their own right: one year later: report of the follow-up interviews with carers of people with learning disabilities in five local authorities in the south west of England*, Norah Fry Research Centre: University of Bristol.

Routledge, M. (2000) Collective responsibilities, fragmented systems: transition to adulthood for young people with learning disabilities, *Tizard Learning Disability Review* 5, 4, 17–26.

Russell, O., Simons, K., Lauruol, J & Foster, J. (1996) *Quantifying the needs and looking towards the future: a survey of the health and social care needs of people with learning difficulties living in Bristol and district*, Norah Fry Research Centre: University of Bristol.

Sanderson, H., Kennedy, J., Ritchie, P. & Goodwin, G. (1997) *People, plans and possibilities*, Scottish Human Services (SHS): Edinburgh.

Simons, K. (2001) *Strategies for change. 'Developing housing and support options' briefing papers: introduction and context setting*, Norah Fry Research Centre: Bristol. *http://www.bristol.ac.uk/Depts/NorahFry/Strategies/*

Simons, K. & Ward, L. (1997) *A foot in the door: the early years of supported living in the UK*, National Development Team: Manchester.

Social Services Inspectorate (1994) *Growing up and moving on: report of an SSI project on transition services for disabled young people*, Department of Health: London.

Social Services Inspectorate (1995) *Opportunities or knocks: national inspection of recreation and leisure in day services for people with learning difficulties*, Department of Health: London.

Swain, J. & Thirlaway, C. (1994) Families in transition. In: S. French (ed.) *On equal terms: working with disabled people*, Butterworth-Heinemann: Oxford.

Wood, A. & Hall, C. (2001) *Your place to live – making it happen*, Mencap: Ealing.

Appendix 1: The composition of the sample

Fifty-three per cent of the young people covered by the postal survey were male and 47% female. Just over a third were still at secondary school (38%); the remainder had already left school.

The majority of the young people in the survey were white (97%) with just a handful being described as Asian or Asian British, mixed or of any other ethnic background. The proportion of ethnic minority respondents is low compared with the proportion of ethnic minority people in the population generally; the Home Farm Trust acknowledges that the database is currently skewed to a predominantly White client group.

Evidence suggests that the problems outlined in this report are likely to be worse for Black and ethnic minority families (Mir et al, 2001), with their needs being poorly met and services for them leaving much to be desired (Baxter et al, 1990; Chamba et al, 1999; Azmi et al 1996). Recent work undertaken specifically on transition in Lambeth, Lewisham and Southwark confirms that the problems experienced are heightened for families from Black and minority ethnic communities (Khan et al, 1998). Parents/carers with English as a second language had little access to interpreting services, and the young people themselves often had to translate at interviews with professionals. The need for professionals to have increased awareness of the cumulative impact on individuals of racism, disadvantage and disability – and how this affects people's experiences of services – was highlighted.

Appendix 2: The development of the *Growing Up* workbook

Workbooks called *Growing Up* were developed in consultation with groups of young people with learning difficulties. These were then used to guide the young people's interviews.

The consultation process and the development of the workbooks took several weeks. During this time, two focus groups were held with young people already attending Transition Projects. A letter was sent to each of the Projects, explaining the research and requesting the help of the young people. The young people themselves were asked to consent to take part in the focus groups; the Project Leaders were asked not to consent on their behalf. A convenient time and place for each group was then arranged, and one of the research team (PH) guided each focus group. Both were tape-recorded with the agreement of all of the young people. At the end of the focus groups, each of the participants was offered a gift voucher (from a place of their own choice) as a token of thanks for their help.

The first focus group was of four young people with learning difficulties who used a Transitions Project in North West England. They were accompanied by the Transition Project Worker and a local advocacy worker. Prior to the focus group, the young people had met with the Transition Project Worker and discussed what questions they thought might be asked in interviews with other young people about their experiences at transition. At the focus group meeting itself, the young people related some of the content of these discussions, and then concentrated on the issue of how best to engage young people with learning difficulties in an interview and what materials might be appropriate to use.

The second focus group was with five young people attending a Transition Project for young disabled people from ethnic minorities in London. They were accompanied by two Transition Project Workers, one from their own project and one from a neighbouring Transition Project, two support workers and one sibling who acted as a sign language interpreter. The young people were familiar with all of these people. The focus group was held as part of an evening activities session. The discussions were mainly about what the most important issues were for the young people as they grew up, what some of the best or worst aspects of growing up were, and what aspects of growing up and leaving school young people might worry about. These then became the topic subjects for the interviews with young people in the study.

Following the focus groups, a variety of materials were devised and piloted to determine which were most accessible, and clear, for young people with learning difficulties. The intention was that the materials would guide any discussion with young people about their experiences of growing up and leaving school. Two young people with learning difficulties in their last year at a local residential school helped pilot the materials. This took place over several meetings, and involved spending social time together, as well as simply looking at the transition materials. One of the young people used some speech; one used Makaton, gestures, symbols and pictures to communicate. At the end of the piloting, both youngsters were thanked with a gift voucher each of their choice.

During the piloting, booklets of different sizes and materials using questions, pictures, symbols and photographs about growing up were tried out. Smaller sized booklets and those using symbols were found to be least popular. The most popular materials were those that gave the young people something to do, as well as something to look at and communicate about. They were of bright, sturdy design with simple, clear, colourful pictures. Each main question was illustrated, as were a number of 'prompts' that gave possible responses to the questions.

As a result of the piloting, an A4 size booklet called *Growing Up* was refined. It had a laminated, bright yellow front cover, was ring bound and made of sturdy paper. At the front were pictures of young people at different stages of growing up, to introduce the concept. There was also space for the young person to personalise the book by sticking in photographs of themselves at various stages of growing up. The remainder of the book asked questions about growing up and offered illustrated suggestions for answers. For each open page, there was one question and a series of illustrated suggestions for answers. The young people indicated their answers using bright, easy-to-handle stickers that were placed in the book. Each young person chose their stickers from a selection of designs at the beginning of the interview. They were encouraged to talk about their choices and about any other thoughts that they had and to write or draw in their books. At the end of the book, they could add any further comments that they wanted to about 'growing up' using speech bubble stickers. All of the young people were given their *Growing Up* books and any unused stickers to keep at the end of the interview, if they wished.

Appendix 3: Contact details

Acting Up (See Multi Media Profiling below)

APASENTH (Asian Parents Association for Special Educational Needs in Tower Hamlets)
Contact: Mahmud Hason
Address: The Brady Centre, 192–196 Hanbury Street, London E1 5HU
Tel: 020 7375 0554
Email: apasenth@btconnect.com

Barnardo's Connect Project
Contact: John Drury
Address: Barnardo's Queens Road Project, Queens Road, Bradford BD8 7BS
Tel: 01274 481183
Email: john.drury@barnardos.org.uk

Barnardo's Supported Lodgings for Young People
Contact: Gill Keighley
Address: Grove Road Project, Barnardo's Services Ltd, 37a Grove Road, Harrogate, North Yorkshire HG1 5EW
Tel: 01423 524149
Email: gill.keighley@barnardos.org.uk

Bournemouth and Poole College
Contact: Denise Woodford
Address: Workforce & Business Development, Room 225, Bournemouth and Poole College, North Road, Parkstone, Poole, Dorset BH14 0LS
Tel: 01202 205950
Email: dwoodford@bpc.ac.uk

Dr B's Restaurant and Coffee Shop
Contact: Nadine Good
Address: 13–15 Knaresborough Road, Harrogate, North Yorkshire HG2 7SR
Tel: 01423 884819
Email: drbs.harrogate@barnardos.org.uk

The Eastern Region (SEN) Partnership Project:
Contact: Jackie Jackson-Smith
Tel: 01245 436320
Email: jackie.jackson-smith@essexcc.gov.uk
Website: www.hertsdirect.org/senregionalproject

East Surrey Transition Project (now county-wide as Partnership with Parents)
Contact: Jonathan Brown (County Transition Adviser)
Address: Partnership with Parents, c/o Furzefield Primary School, Delabole Road, Merstham, Surrey, RH1 3PA
Tel: 01737 646227
Email: jonathan.brown@surreycc.gov.uk

The Home Farm Trust – Transition Workshops for Parents and Siblings
Contact: Robina Mallett, Carer Support Worker
Address: Merchants House North, Wapping Road, Bristol BS1 4RW
Tel: 0117 930 2608
Website: www.hft.org.uk
Email: robina@hft.org.uk

MENCAP's Trans-active Project
Contact: Claire Brown
Address: 4 Swan Courtyard, Coventry Road, Birmingham, B26 1BU
Tel: 0121 707 7877 ext.223
Website: www.trans-active.org.uk

Multimedia Profiling with Acting Up
Contact: John Ladle
Address: Acting Up, Unit 304, Mare Street Studios, 203–213 Mare Street, London E8 3QE
Tel: 02085 333344
Website: www.acting-up.org.uk
Email: acting-up@geo2.poptel.org.uk

Oldham Learning Disability Service
Contact: Ken Stapleton, Team Manager for Care Management and Social Work in the Adult Learning Disability Services OMBC
Address: Broadway House, Broadway Chatterton, Oldham, OL9 8RW
Tel: 0161 911 3868
Email: socs.ldbroadwayhouse@oldham.gov.uk

Plymouth Social and Housing Services
Contact: Transitions Coordinator – Sioux
Crudington
Address: Plymouth City Council, Windsor
House, Plymouth, PL1 2AA
Tel: 01752 307314 ext. 7514
Email: sioux.crudington@plymouth.gov.uk

Status Employment
Contact: Chief executive – Peter Farrel
Address: 6 West Way Gardens, Shirley,
Croydon, Surrey, CR0 8RA
Tel: 020 8655 3344
Email: status_emp@msn.com

Sunfield School's Family Charter
Contact: Sally Conway, Coordinator for Family
Services
Address: Sunfield, Clent Grove, Clent,
Stourbridge, Worcs DY9 9PB
Tel: 01562 882 253
Email: sallyc@sunfieldsch.worc.co.uk

Surrey Strategic Planning
Contact: Kathy Taylor, Service Development
Manager for Children with
Disabilities
Address: Surrey Children's Services, Surrey
County Council, County Hall,
Penrhyn Road, Kingston, Surrey, KT1
2DN
Tel: 020 8541 8527
Email: Kathy.taylor@surreycc.gov.uk

**Surrey Users Network 'communication passports'
(now called Clear Communication People Ltd)**
Contact: Mike Leat
Address: Astolat, Coniers Way, Burpham,
Guildford, GU4 7HL
Tel: 01483 447402
Email: mike.leat@talk21.com

The Trans-active Project, Mencap
Contact: Claire Brown
Address: 4 Swan Courtyard, Coventry Road,
Birmingham, B26 1BU
Tel: 0121 707 7877 ext 223
Website: www.trans-active.org.uk